KEDA BLACK

BATCH COOKING

PHOTOGRAPHY PIERRE JAVELLE
STYLIST CHRISTINE LEGERET

Hardie Grant

BOOKS

CONTENTS

What is batch cooking? page 5

How to use this book page 6

Practical tips page 8

Seasonal produce page 10

Week 1 page 12

Beef stew with potatoes and salad
Caesar salad with garlic bread
Spicy chickpeas, tomatoes and spinach with rice
Tagliatelle with beef sauce, sundried tomatoes and spinach
Squash and sweet potato soup with garlic bread
Crème caramel

Week 2 page 24

Pear and blue cheese mini pizzas with salad
Big broccoli and lentil salad with peanut dressing
Thai noodles
Autumn-winter gratin with blue cheese
Lemongrass, coconut, coriander and ginger soup
Peanut-choc cookies

Week 3 page 36

Baked eggs with mushrooms
Roast autumn vegetables with mozzarella
Spaghetti with meatballs
Cabbage, fennel and mozzarella pizza
Cabbage and split pea soup with meatballs
Bread pudding

Week 4 page 48

One-pot pasta with cauliflower, lemon, Cheddar and rosemary
Broccoli flans with salad
Cream of vegetable soup
Vegetable curry with rice
Camembert and potatoes with salad
Baked apples

Week 5 page 60

Poached chicken breasts, carrots and potatoes with
  pomegranate condiment
Onion and blue cheese puff pastry tart with watercress salad
Noodles with vegetables and chicken
Fried eggs, onions and chilli with salad
Watercress soup
Pancakes

Week 6 page 72

Beef stew with persillade
Next-day beef stew salad
Risotto
Noodles in beef stew stock with lemongrass sauce
Croque monsieur with salad
Shortbread biscuits

Week 7 page 84

Chicken tikka kebabs with rocket
Goat's cheese and herb omelette with rocket
Chicken biryani with cranberries
Rice bowl, roast broccoli and yoghurt dressing
Herb and ravioli soup
Granola

Week 8 page 96

Fish gratin with lettuce
Pasta, fennel, orange and cashew salad
Ham quiche with lettuce
Pasta with garlic-infused oil, cucumber salad
  and yoghurt dressing
Pea soup with garlic crostini
Scones

Week 9 page 108

Hake, green beans and radishes with pesto and bulgur
Swiss chard tarts with cherry tomatoes
Pasta with pesto
Vegetable couscous with merguez
Pistou soup
Baked rhubarb

Week 10 page 120

Chicken tabbouleh
Gazpacho and hummus
Green shakshuka with feta
Summer vegetable pasta
Gratin with sardines
Raspberry clafoutis

Week 11 page 132

Rice bowl, courgette fritters and aubergine-yoghurt dressing
Focaccia with lettuce
Vegetable lasagne
Fried rice, saffron and apricots with tomato salad
Red shakshuka
Milkshake

Week 12 page 144

Salade Niçoise
Stuffed vegetables
Olive and goat's cheese pasta with buttered radishes
Avocado and fried rice
Sage ravioli with cucumber
Roasted fruit

Week 13 page 156

Roast chicken, vegetables and tortilla wraps
Omelette with buttered radishes
Fried rice with chicken
Red lentil and coconut milk soup with tuna parcels
Carbonara
Pear brownies

Create your own batch page 168

Index page 182

Labels for photocopying page 185

WHAT IS BATCH COOKING?

Simply put, the idea is to prepare meals for the whole week in advance. After doing the shopping, you will need to spend around 2 hours in the kitchen on a Sunday getting the bulk of the work done. Then all you have to do each evening is spend around 10 minutes putting together the finishing touches to the meal.

3

Three good reasons for taking up batch cooking

MAKING LIFE EASIER

It's great if you can do a little shopping every day or make something up from what you happen to have in the refrigerator, but it's not always easy to find time to do this during the week. With batch cooking, all your meals are planned and can be ready in no time.

EATING WELL AND EATING ONLY HOMEMADE FOOD

Getting organised means you can provide a home-cooked meal every day, however simple, instead of resorting to ready meals, frozen foods or ordering takeaways too often.

LESS WASTE

You use everything you buy. You cook fresh produce sooner, especially vegetables, which then take up less space in the refrigerator and don't end up rotting in the vegetable compartment.

HOW TO USE THIS BOOK

1. Menu of the week

List of the week's dishes

Tip for vegetarians

Time in the kitchen on Sunday

The best season for this menu

Storage containers

2. Sunday's results

In the photo: all the food you will have ready at the end of your Sunday prep session

Cooking utensils

Tip for changing an ingredient

3. Visual shopping guide

Week number reference label

All the ingredients you need in their different categories

Photo of each ingredient

Basic storecupboard ingredients

4. Steps to follow on Sunday

Each step of cooking is numbered to help you get organised

Clear visuals to illustrate each step of the cooking process

The time taken by each step

At the end of each step, follow the advice for storing the food you have prepared.

THE INSTRUCTIONS

→ **CLING FILM:**
cover with cling film (plastic wrap)

→ **CONTAINER:**
put in a container

→ **TEA TOWEL:**
wrap in a tea (dish) towel

→ **FREEZER BAG:**
put in a bag

→ **REFRIGERATOR:**
store in the refrigerator

→ **FREEZER:**
store in the freezer

→ **CUPBOARD:**
keep in a storecupboard at room temperature

5. For every weekday evening

Photo of the finished dish

Name of the dish

Prep time

What is left to do

What to do for the next day

PRACTICAL TIPS

CONTAINERS

Tubs and jars

Use glass rather than plastic where possible: glass lasts a lifetime and plastic may contain toxic chemicals that can be transferred to the food, especially when the food contains fat or is hot. If using plastic, choose classification types #2, #4 and #5 as these are normally non-toxic.

For freezing, use plastic. Liquids increase in volume as they freeze, and this can cause a glass container to crack.

Bowls and other dishes

You can also use mixing bowls, salad bowls and other dishes – and cover with a plate or homemade beeswax fabric (you can find tutorials on YouTube), rather than using large quantities of cling film (plastic wrap) or aluminium foil.

This is the simplest and most economical solution, but it can be less practical since your prepped foods might take up a lot of room in the refrigerator.

Freezer bags

Reusable bags are very practical for herbs or salads and improve their longevity. They are suitable for 'clean', non-fatty foods, after which you can easily reuse them. For other types of food, it's best to use containers that are easy to wash.

How many containers do I need?

For each menu in this book, you will need on average:
- 4–5 × 300 ml (10 fl oz/1¼ cups) containers
- 4–5 × 750 ml (25 fl oz/3 cups) containers
- 4–5 × 1.5 litres (51 fl oz/6 cups) containers
- several small jars or tubs

You can recycle jam (jelly) pots and packaging. Beware of plastic containers that may not be suitable for putting in the dishwasher or for containing fats.

TIMING AND QUANTITIES

Quantities

The menus in this book are designed to serve 4. Obviously, appetites vary and so do family sizes, so don't hesitate to adjust the quantities up or down, add a bread and cheese course, or even some fruit and yoghurt for dessert.

Timing

Approximate timings are given for each menu and stage. These times may vary greatly from one person to another. Some cooks are slow and some are quick; some clear and wash up as they go; some are new to cooking; others are old hands … In any case, you will find that you can do an enormous amount in an hour or two, and you'll get quicker with practise.

And what to do with any leftovers?

You can freeze any leftovers (but do not refreeze a dish you have defrosted), turn them into soups, add them to your lunch box, or serve them up the next day in a different form. It's almost always possible to avoid throwing food away!

HOW TO PRESERVE THE FOOD YOU HAVE PREPARED

There is no absolute rule when it comes to preserving food. The main thing is to trust your senses; smell and taste the foods, etc. It is important to be careful with perishable ingredients: no longer than 2 days for preparations containing raw egg, or perishable products such as meat, fish or cold cuts. Vegetables carry less risk, apart from some deterioration in taste.

What can you keep in the refrigerator?

- Stewed dishes and stuffed vegetables will keep in the refrigerator for several days. They will improve in flavour.
- Dips and condiments keep very well because of the fat they contain: cover pesto and other relishes with a layer of oil.
- Chilled rice dries out slightly in the refrigerator; just what you need for fried rice! Root vegetables (potatoes, carrots,

etc.), once peeled, will keep for 2 or 3 days, but immerse them in cold water to prevent browning.

■ Onions sweated in butter or oil keep very well for a few days and even longer when frozen.

■ Salad leaves and fresh herbs, washed and spun, keep very well in a tub, jar or freezer bag. With lettuce, remove the leaves with care so as not to break them: it is when they are damaged that they turn brown and rot. They like to have a little moisture but not too much.

■ Acidic, sweet or savoury seasonings tend to 'cook' foods, so store them separately and add them at the last minute.

Is it necessary to have a freezer?

■ A freezer is a useful ally: it preserves certain nutrients well, not to mention flavour. Soups freeze well and retain their vitamins better. It's better to freeze them than leave them for 2–3 days in the refrigerator.

■ It is best to freeze perishable products such as meat and fish to increase their life. There is nothing to stop you from buying meats close to their use-by date and freezing them immediately.

■ Please note that freezing does impair the texture of certain items, particularly many raw vegetables, because when the water they contain freezes it breaks their structure.

How to defrost?

It is always best to defrost an item slowly by placing it in the refrigerator on the day before you need it, rather than reheating it directly, whether in the oven, on the hob or in the microwave.

SOME ALTERNATIVES TO PROCESSED PRODUCTS

In this book, we have chosen to emphasise very simple cooking. Batch cooking enables you to rationalise your work and so use mainly fresh and raw products. This is a healthier way to eat, avoiding all the additives and sugars that go into ready meals and processed foods. Some ready-made products are, however, very convenient and can save you a lot of time. Here are a few tips to avoid consuming industrially-processed food.

Pastry and bread dough

Make your own shortcrust pastry or bread dough. If you are not going to use it straight away, just roll it out and freeze it. For pizzas, use ready-made pizza bases from the supermarket.

Stock

It's really easy to make your own stock. Put a few vegetables, seasonings and the leftover bones and skin from a chicken carcass into a pot, cover with water and simmer for a few hours. Strain and leave to cool. Homemade stock keeps for 1 week in the refrigerator or 1 month in the freezer. In the meantime, you can use stock cubes, but choose organic ones as they do not contain unnecessary additives or flavour enhancers.

You're a fan of frozen foods?

This is not incompatible with batch cooking. For example, if you hate peeling and slicing onions because it makes you cry and you're passing the frozen food store, get them ready prepared.

SEASONAL PRODUCE

Autumn

Vegetables

Beetroot (beet)
Broccoli (end of the season)
Cabbage (all types)
Carrots
Celery and celeriac (celery root)
Fennel
Garlic
Leeks
Marrows (all types)
Onions
Parsnips
Potatoes
Spinach
Sweetcorn
Swiss chard (more of a springtime vegetable
    but sometimes available in winter)
Tomatoes
Turnips
Winter salads: chicory (endive), frisée, lamb's lettuce,
    escarole, etc.

Fruit and nuts

Apples
Blueberries
Chestnuts
Clementines (in December)
Figs (in October)
Grapes
Hazelnuts
Kiwi fruit
Lemons
Mandarins
Oranges (in December)
Pears
Quince
Raspberries (in October)
Walnuts

Winter

Vegetables

Beetroot (beet)
Cabbage (all types)
Carrots
Celery and celeriac (celery root)
Garlic
Leeks
Marrows (all types)
Onions
Parsnips and other root vegetables
Potatoes
Sweetcorn
Swiss chard (more of a springtime vegetable
    but sometimes available in winter)
Turnips
Winter salads: chicory (endive), frisée, lamb's lettuce,
    escarole, etc.

By all means include frozen peas and beans and use
good tinned or bottled tomatoes for sauces.

Fruit and nuts

Apples
Clementines
Grapefruits
Kiwi fruit
Lemons
Mandarins
Oranges
Pears

IT'S IN SEASON!

Eating what's in season means you're getting the freshest produce
that's travelled the smallest distance to you plate, as well as varying
your diet based on availability throughout the year. It's good for
you and the environment. Please note, these seasonal produce lists
are based on availability in the Northern Hemisphere. If you live
elsewhere, please consult local seasonality information for more
relevant guidance.

Spring

Vegetables

Artichokes
Asparagus
Broccoli
Cauliflower
Celery
Courgettes (zucchini)
Cucumber
Early beetroot (beet)
Early turnips
Fennel
French beans, runner beans, beans for shelling
Green garlic
New potatoes
Peas and broad (fava) beans
Potatoes
Radishes
Spinach
Spring onions (scallions)
Spring salads: lettuce, rocket (arugula), etc.
Swiss chard
Young carrots
Young leeks

Fruit and nuts

Apricots
Blackcurrants
Cherries
Gooseberries
Grapefruit
Rhubarb
Strawberries
Watermelon

Summer

Vegetables

Artichokes
Aubergines (eggplant)
Bell peppers
Broccoli
Celery
Courgettes (zucchini)
Cucumber
Early carrots
French beans, runner beans
Green garlic
New potatoes
Potatoes
Radishes
Spinach
Spring onions (scallions)
Summer salads: lettuce, etc.
Sweetheart cabbage
Swiss chard
Tomatoes

Fruit and nuts

Apricots
Blackberries
Blackcurrants
Blueberries
Figs
Gooseberries
Grapes
Hazelnuts
Melon
Nectarines
Peaches
Plums
Raspberries
Strawberries
Walnuts
Watermelon

FROM MARCH TO SEPTEMBER...

This is very much the best time, when vegetables are easy to use and require little preparation, cooking or seasoning. There is no need to peel vegetables: if their skin is very thin, just scrub and rinse. If you have a surfeit of herbs or other salad leaves (watercress, rocket), make different kinds of pesto (this also works with those lovely radish tops). You can also freeze them for later use in cooked preparations or soups

This is also the time for garnishes made from finely diced fresh, cooked or raw vegetables, seasoned with more strongly flavoured produce, such as olives, garlic, herbs, drizzled with oil and sprinkled with a little salt, which will add flavour to the simplest foods, such as soup, fried eggs, etc.

Week 01

Monday
Beef stew with potatoes and salad

Tuesday
Caesar salad with garlic bread

Wednesday
Spicy chickpeas, tomatoes and spinach with rice

Thursday
Tagliatelle with beef sauce, sundried tomatoes and spinach

Friday
Squash and sweet potato soup with garlic bread

Special treat
Crème caramel

TIMING 🕐

1 H 30
MINUTES IN THE KITCHEN

SEASON: AUTUMN

Out of season, substitute the squash with courgettes (zucchini). In spring, use fresh spinach.

VEGETARIAN

Substitute the stew with vegetable couscous (week 9) and the beef sauce with the olive and goat's cheese dressing (week 12).

IF YOU DON'T LIKE

Spinach: substitute with rocket (arugula).

For storing

2 containers about 300 ml
(10 fl oz/1¼ cups)
1 container about 750 ml
(25 fl oz/3 cups)
4 containers about 1.5 litres
(51 fl oz/6 cups)
1 tea (dish) towel or freezer bag

Utensils

1 food processor
1 hand-held blender
baking parchment
and string
1 small saucepan
1 mould, diameter 20–
25 cm (8–10 in)

1 oven dish
1 large saucepan
1 frying (skillet) or
sauté pan
1 casserole dish
(Dutch oven)

THURSDAY

MONDAY

TUESDAY

FRIDAY

WEDNESDAY

SPECIAL TREAT

Fruit, vegetables and herbs

- ❏ 3 medium-sized sweet potatoes
- ❏ 1 large seasonal lettuce
- ❏ 1 small squash (1 kg/2 lb 3 oz)
- ❏ 10 garlic cloves
- ❏ 2 carrots
- ❏ 5 onions
- ❏ 1 lemon
- ❏ 1 large bunch of flat-leaf parsley
- ❏ 1 kg (2 lb 4 oz) potatoes

Frozen foods

- ❏ 1 kg (2 lb 4 oz) frozen spinach

Baked goods

- ❏ 2 baguettes

Chilled produce

- ❏ 1.5 kg (3 lb 5 oz) beef: chuck steak and/ or shin of beef (a little more if it's on the bone), sliced
- ❏ 1.2 litres (40 fl oz/ 4¾ cups) full-fat (whole) milk
- ❏ 60 g (2 oz) Parmesan
- ❏ 300 g (10½ oz) Greek-style yoghurt
- ❏ 100 g (3½ oz) butter
- ❏ 13–17 eggs

General groceries

- ❏ 4 × 400 g (14 oz) tins peeled or chopped tomatoes
- ❏ 2 × 400 g (14 oz) tins chickpeas (garbanzos)
- ❏ 100 g (3½ oz) sundried tomatoes
- ❏ 1 × 100 g (3½ oz) jar anchovy fillets (in oil or brine), rinsed well
- ❏ 2 organic vegetable stock cubes
- ❏ 1 vanilla pod (bean)
- ❏ 240 g (8½ oz/1¼ cups) basmati rice or long-grain rice
- ❏ 400 g (14 oz) tagliatelle
- ❏ 300 ml (10 fl oz/1¼ cups) passata (sieved tomatoes)
- ❏ 150 g (5 oz/1 cup) black olives

Storecupboard

- ❏ mustard
- ❏ caster (superfine) sugar
- ❏ salt and pepper
- ❏ Indian spice mix: garam masala, curry
- ❏ olive oil
- ❏ vinegar of your choice
- ❏ coarse salt
- ❏ 3 sprigs of dried thyme or oregano

1. Advance preparation

🕐 20 minutes

Take the butter out of the refrigerator to soften it.
Scrub the squash. Wash and drain the parsley. Peel the carrots, potatoes and sweet potatoes.
Cut the carrots, sweet potatoes and squash into large cubes.
Wash the potatoes. Cut into large cubes and immerse in cold water (to prevent browning). → **CONTAINER → REFRIGERATOR**
Wash and drain the salad. → **TEA (DISH) TOWEL → REFRIGERATOR**
Peel the garlic and onions. Slice the onions thinly. Separate the parsley leaves from the stalks. → **CONTAINER OR TEA (DISH) TOWEL →**
REFRIGERATOR Keep the stalks.

2. Garlic bread

🕐 15 minutes

Preheat the oven to 150°C (300°F/Gas 1).
THE GARLIC BUTTER Blend a third of the parsley in a food processor with 2 grated garlic cloves and the softened butter.
THE BAGUETTES Halve the baguettes, then cut notches 2–3 cm (around 1 in) deep in each half. Spread herb butter in each gap. Wrap the baguette halves two by two in baking parchment and tie with string. Put one of the wrapped baguettes in the freezer. Bake the other one in the oven for 30–40 minutes. Leave to cool, open the bag, separate the slices and store them in the paper or in a container. → **CUPBOARD**

3. Crème caramel

🕐 20 minutes

THE CARAMEL Put 200 g (7 oz/scant 1 cup) sugar in a small saucepan with just enough water to moisten it. Heat carefully until the sugar begins to turn a caramel colour (170°C/340°F on the thermometer). Prepare a container or sink with cold water and immerse the bottom of the saucepan as soon as the caramel is ready to stop it cooking further. Be very careful not to burn yourself! Pour into a mould and tilt on all sides, holding it by the edges to coat the bottom with caramel.
THE MILK Heat 1 litre (34 fl oz/4 cups) milk in a saucepan with the vanilla pod split in half. Break 8 eggs into a large bowl, add 150 g (5 oz/scant ¾ cup) sugar and beat until light and pale. Scrape the vanilla seeds into the milk with a knife (rinse the pod, leave it to dry and put it in a jar of sugar).
COOKING Pour the almost-boiling milk onto the sweetened eggs and beat. Pour the mixture into the mould. Stand it in a deep baking tray (pan) and fill the tray up to halfway with hot water around the mould. Bake for 40 minutes at 150°C (300°F/Gas 1) until the top is golden brown. Leave to cool.
→ **COVER WITH CLING FILM (PLASTIC WRAP) →**
REFRIGERATOR Eat within 3 days.

4. Chickpeas

 10 minutes

THE ONIONS Take out a large saucepan for the soup, a frying pan (skillet) or sauté pan for the chickpea (garbanzo) dish and a casserole dish (Dutch oven) for the stew. Pour 3 tablespoons of oil into the dish and add the onions with a pinch of salt. Cook over a medium-low heat for 6–7 minutes. Divide the onions among the three pans: a third for the soup, a third for the chickpeas and the remaining third in the casserole dish.

THE TOMATOES AND CHICKPEAS Heat a frying pan over a medium heat, add 2 grated garlic cloves, stir for 1 minute, add 2 teaspoons of Indian spice mix, season with salt and stir again. Add 2 tins of tomatoes, stir, crushing the tomatoes with the wooden spoon if they are whole. Add the drained chickpeas, lower the heat and simmer for about 10 minutes. Allow to cool. ➔ **CONTAINER** ➔ **REFRIGERATOR**

5. Soup

 20 minutes

Heat the saucepan for the soup over a medium heat, add the sweet potatoes, one carrot and the squash cut into cubes, stir and cook for 1–2 minutes. Add water to cover, 2 stock cubes and almost all of the parsley stalks. Bring to a simmer, cover and cook for 25 minutes over a low heat. Add the remaining half of the parsley leaves to the soup and blend, adding the remaining milk. Season with salt and pepper to taste. Allow the soup to cool.
➔ **CONTAINER** ➔ **FREEZER**

6. Stew

20 minutes

THE STEW In the casserole dish (Dutch oven) put the meat, 7 anchovy fillets, 5 grated garlic cloves, 2 tins of tomatoes and the passata (sieved tomatoes), a pinch of sugar, 3 sprigs of thyme or oregano, the remaining parsley stalks, two-thirds of the olives and 1 carrot cut into cubes. Cover and bring to a simmer on the hob then put in the oven for 3–4 hours, lowering the temperature to 140°C (275°F/Gas ½). (You can forget about it and do something else meanwhile as it needs no intervention). It is done when the meat is tender. Allow to cool completely. ➔ **CASSEROLE DISH OR CONTAINER** ➔ **REFRIGERATOR**
THE BEEF SAUCE Take a quarter of this cooked stew, chop it with the knife along with the sundried tomatoes, the remaining olives and a handful of parsley.
➔ **CONTAINER** ➔ **REFRIGERATOR**

7. Caesar dressing

5 minutes

Break an egg into the food processor bowl, add a grated garlic clove, 2 teaspoons lemon juice, 2 anchovy fillets, 1 teaspoon mustard and one-third of the remaining parsley. Blend in the food processor, then gradually add, with the blender still running, 150 ml (5 fl oz/scant ⅔ cup) olive oil mixed with 1 tablespoon of the oil from the anchovies. If you do not have a food processor or blender, make the dressing with a whisk, leaving aside the anchovies; chop the anchovies very finely and add them to the dressing. Season with pepper.
➔ **CONTAINER** ➔ **REFRIGERATOR** Use a peeler to shave off Parmesan strips. ➔ **CONTAINER** ➔ **REFRIGERATOR**

Beef stew with potatoes and salad

🕐 Ready in 30 minutes, including 10 minutes prep

THE STEW Reheat the stew over a medium-low heat.

THE POTATOES Drain the refrigerated potatoes, put in a saucepan and cover well with cold water and some coarse salt. Bring to a medium boil and cook for 20–25 minutes until tender. Serve the stew with the potatoes and side salad.

Caesar salad with garlic bread

🕐 Ready in 20 minutes, including 10 minutes prep

THE EGGS Put 4 eggs (or 8 if you're really hungry) into a saucepan, cover with water, bring to a boil and cook for 4 minutes. Remove the eggs, rinse in cold water and remove the shell.

THE SALAD Tear the salad leaves and arrange in a bowl.

FINISHING THE SALAD Drizzle the salad with the dressing, toss well and add the eggs, halved, a few anchovies and strips of Parmesan (save some for Thursday). Eat with the garlic bread.

FOR WEDNESDAY AND THURSDAY Take the spinach out of the freezer and put in the refrigerator to defrost.

Wednesday

Spicy chickpeas, tomatoes and spinach with rice

🕐 Ready in 25 minutes, including 10 minutes prep

THE RICE Measure the quantity of rice in a glass and heat in a saucepan with 1.5 times its volume of water and ½ teaspoon salt. Bring to the boil, then lower the heat to minimum, close tightly with a lid and cook for 11 minutes. Remove the lid, stir gently with a fork and place a clean tea (dish) towel over the rice.

THE CHICKPEAS Reheat the chickpea (garbanzo) mixture. When it's hot, add two-thirds of the defrosted spinach, stir and cook until heated through. Sprinkle with parsley.

THE YOGHURT Mix the Greek-style yoghurt with a good pinch of Indian spice mix and serve the chickpeas and spinach with the yoghurt.

Tagliatelle with beef sauce, sundried tomatoes and spinach

🕐 Ready in 25 minutes, including 10 minutes prep

THE SAUCE Reheat the beef sauce and add the remaining spinach.

THE PASTA Boil the tagliatelle for the time stated on the packet in boiling salted water. Drain and pour into the beef sauce. Stir well and serve with the strips of Parmesan.

FOR FRIDAY Take the soup and garlic bread out of the freezer and defrost in the refrigerator.

Squash and sweet potato soup with garlic bread

🕐 Ready in 25 minutes, including 5 minutes prep

Preheat the oven to 190°C (375°F/gas 5) and bake the garlic bread for 20 minutes. In the meantime, reheat the soup. Sprinkle with parsley. Serve the soup with the bread.

Crème caramel

🕐 Already prepared

Run a knife round the mould between the crème and the side. Lay a plate on the mould and turn over, tapping once (but not too hard!) to release it.

Week 02

Monday
Pear and blue cheese mini pizzas with salad

Tuesday
Big broccoli and lentil salad with peanut dressing

Wednesday
Thai noodles

Thursday
Autumn–winter gratin with blue cheese

Friday
Lemongrass, coconut, coriander and ginger soup

Special treat
Peanut-choc cookies

TIMING 🕐

1 H 40
MINUTES IN THE KITCHEN

SEASON: AUTUMN–WINTER

Out of season, substitute this gratin with the summer gratin (week 10).

IF YOU DON'T LIKE

Blue cheese: substitute with Comté or other melting cheese.

For storing

3 containers about 300 ml
(10 fl oz/1¼ cups)
4 containers about 750 ml
(25 fl oz/3 cups)
1 container about 2 litres (70 fl oz/8 cups)
1 tea (dish) towel

Utensils

1 baking tray (pan)
1 oven dish
1 steamer
1 medium saucepan
1 large stewpot
1 food processor or 1 pestle and mortar
1 large frying pan (skillet) or wok

WEDNESDAY

SPECIAL TREAT

TUESDAY

FRIDAY

MONDAY

THURSDAY

Fruit, vegetables and herbs

❏ 1 large cos (romaine) lettuce (or 2 medium sized)

❏ 3 heads of broccoli

❏ 6 shallots

❏ 7 garlic cloves

❏ 1 sweet potato

❏ 13 cm (5 in) ginger root

❏ 3 small stalks and leaves of Swiss chard or pak choi (bok choi) (about 700 g/1 lb 9 oz)

❏ 4 pears

❏ 5 potatoes

❏ 5 carrots

❏ 5 sticks of lemongrass

❏ 2 small chillies (can be substituted with dried chilli (hot pepper) flakes or powder)

❏ 1 lemon

❏ 2 bunches of coriander (cilantro)

❏ 1 bunch of mint

Chilled produce

❏ 250 g (9 oz) gorgonzola (traditional or layered with mascarpone)

❏ 200 ml (7 fl oz/scant 1 cup) crème fraîche

❏ 500–600 g (1 lb 2 oz– 1 lb 5 oz) pizza dough or 2 rounds ready-made pizza dough or 1 packet of shortcrust pastry

❏ 6 eggs

❏ 200 g (7 oz) salted butter

General groceries

- ❑ 200 g (7 oz) rice noodles, preferably flat
- ❑ 150 g (5 oz/¾ cup) green lentils
- ❑ 300 g (10½ oz/1¼ cups) crunchy peanut butter
- ❑ 200 ml (7 fl oz/scant 1 cup) coconut milk
- ❑ 200 g (7 oz) dark chocolate
- ❑ 2 organic vegetable stock cubes
- ❑ 200 g (7 oz/1²/₃ cup) hazelnuts

Storecupboard

- ❑ 340 g (5 oz/2¾ cups) plain (all-purpose) flour
- ❑ 120 ml (4 fl oz/½ cup) cider vinegar
- ❑ olive oil
- ❑ 120 ml (4 fl oz/½ cup) soy sauce
- ❑ nutmeg
- ❑ 250 g (9 oz/1¼ cups) caster (superfine) sugar
- ❑ salt and pepper

1. Advance preparation

🕐 30 minutes

Take the butter out of the refrigerator. Wash and dry the lettuce. **→ TEA (DISH) TOWEL → REFRIGERATOR**

Rinse the broccoli, cut the stalks and set them aside, removing any damaged parts, separate the heads into small florets.

Wash and drain all the herbs. Snip the leaves off one of the bunches of coriander (keep the stalks) and the mint. **→ JAR → REFRIGERATOR**

Thinly slice the tender core of 3 sticks of lemongrass, set aside a third for the dressing and store the rest (for sprinkling on the dishes: salad, noodles, soup). **→ JAR → REFRIGERATOR**

Peel the shallots, thinly slice 2 of them. Peel the ginger (not necessary if organic).

Peel the carrots. Chop 3 carrots into small dice and 2 carrots into 2 or 3 large pieces. **→ CONTAINER → REFRIGERATOR**

Wash the Swiss chard or pak choi (bok choi). Cut the green leaves and ribs into strips. Immerse in boiling salted water for 1 minute, drain and immerse in cold water. Drain again. **→ CONTAINER → REFRIGERATOR**

Peel the potatoes and sweet potato. Cut into fine slices, reserving 1 potato for the soup: cut this into large chunks. Chop 150 g (5 oz/1 cup) hazelnuts and the chocolate separately.

2. Mini pizzas

🕐 15 minutes

Preheat the oven to 230°C (450°F/gas 8). Divide the dough into 4 and roll out each one into a disc. Place on a baking tray (pan) covered with baking parchment. Beat an egg with 150 ml (5 fl oz/scant ⅔ cup) cream, season with salt, pepper and a little freshly grated nutmeg. Peel the pears, cut into slices 1 cm (½ in) thick, removing the core, squeeze a little lemon juice over them and arrange them on the discs of dough. Add 1 tablespoon Swiss chard to each disc. Crumble 150 g (5 oz) gorgonzola on top. Sprinkle over 2 tablespoons chopped hazelnuts. Spread on the egg-cream mixture. Bake in the oven for 10 minutes. Allow to cool. **→ COVER WITH CLING FILM (PLASTIC WRAP) → REFRIGERATOR**

3. Gratin

🕐 5 minutes

Lower the oven temperature to 190°C (375°F/gas 5). Rub an oven dish with a halved garlic clove, grease with some oil and arrange the slices of potatoes, alternating with the sweet potato, season with salt and pepper as you go, interspersed with the par-boiled Swiss chard, 2 sliced shallots and 2 thinly sliced garlic cloves. Drizzle generously with olive oil. Bake for 45 minutes. Allow to cool. **→ COVER WITH CLING FILM (PLASTIC WRAP) → REFRIGERATOR**

4. Lentils and broccoli

🕐 10 minutes

THE BROCCOLI Steam the broccoli florets for no more than 5 minutes (you can also boil in water for 5 minutes). Allow to cool. Store with the Swiss chard if you have any left. **→ CONTAINER → REFRIGERATOR**

THE LENTILS Rinse the lentils, put into a saucepan, cover well with cold water and heat. Add 2 or 3 pieces of carrot, a crushed and unpeeled garlic clove and a few coriander stalks. Bring to the boil and cook for 20 minutes over a medium heat: the lentils should be tender but slightly al dente. Allow to cool and drizzle with a little olive oil. **→ CONTAINER → REFRIGERATOR**

5. Soup

⏱ 10 minutes

THE VEGETABLES Put the remaining large pieces of carrot and potato in a stewpot and add 2 sticks of lemongrass, the vegetable stock cubes, 1 chilli (deseeded if you prefer it milder), 10 cm (4 in) crushed ginger, 2 crushed garlic cloves, 2 peeled shallots and the broccoli stems.

COOKING Pour in just enough water to barely cover the ingredients, bring to a boil and simmer for 20 minutes. Add the whole bunch of coriander and the coconut milk, cook very gently for 5 minutes. Blend or pass through a fine mill. Leave to cool completely.

➔ **CONTAINER** ➔ **FREEZER**

6. Cookies

⏱ 15 minutes

Beat the softened butter, 200 g (7 oz/scant 1 cup) sugar and 250 g (9 oz/1 cup) peanut butter. Incorporate 2 eggs, the sifted flour, then the chocolate and 120 g (4 oz/1 cup) chopped hazelnuts. Divide this dough in half and place each on a sheet of baking parchment. Use the parchment to roll into 2 sausages, and wrap in the parchment.

➔ **FREEZER**

7. Peanut dressing

⏱ 15 minutes

Blend in the food processor (or mix by hand) 120 ml (4 fl oz/½ cup) vinegar, 120 ml (4 fl oz/½ cup) soy sauce, 3 tablespoons sugar, 1 chilli, 2 shallots, a third of the lemongrass, chopped, 3 cm (1¼ in) ginger and a grated garlic clove. Add 2 tablespoons peanut butter and mix by hand. ➔ **CONTAINER OR JAR** ➔ **REFRIGERATOR**

Pear and blue cheese mini pizzas with salad

🕐 Ready in 20 minutes, including 5 minutes prep

THE MINI PIZZAS Set the oven to 180°C (350°F/gas 4). Reheat the mini pizzas for 10 minutes.
THE SALAD Put the lettuce leaves into a bowl (keep a few leaves for Thursday), season with a little salt, pepper, lemon juice and olive oil.

Broccoli and lentil salad with peanut dressing

🕐 Ready in 10 minutes

THE LENTILS AND BROCCOLI Put the lentils into a large bowl, add half the steamed broccoli heads and 1 or 2 tablespoons diced carrots (keep the rest for Wednesday).

THE SEASONING Take half of the peanut dressing and thin with 2–3 tablespoons olive oil. Pour over the salad, stir, add coriander leaves, lemongrass, a few torn mint leaves and the remaining chopped hazelnuts.

Thai noodles

🕐 Ready in 15 minutes

THE NOODLES Cook the noodles according to the instructions on the packet (they are all different), drain and rinse with cold water.

THE EGGS AND VEGETABLES Take 3 eggs from the refrigerator, the remaining broccoli/Swiss chard and peanut butter dressing, the herbs and diced carrots. Heat 2 tablespoons oil in a frying pan or large wok over a high heat. Break the eggs into it and cook, stirring continuously. Add the vegetables and stir for 2 minutes.

THE SEASONING Add the noodles and cook for 2 minutes, stirring. Add the peanut butter dressing and stir well. Sprinkle with the the herbs (keep a little for the soup on Friday) and serve.

Autumn-winter gratin with blue cheese

🕐 Ready in 1 hour, including 5 minutes prep

Preheat the oven to 180°C (350°F/gas 4). Bake the gratin for 45 minutes. Serve with bread, the remaining gorgonzola and a few salad leaves, seasoned with a dash of olive oil.

FOR FRIDAY Put the soup in the refrigerator to defrost.

Lemongrass, coconut, coriander and ginger soup

🕐 Ready in 15 minutes, including 5 minutes prep

Reheat the soup on a low heat and sprinkle with the remaining herbs. Serve with bread.

Peanut-choc cookies

🕐 Ready in 15 minutes, including 5 minutes prep

SHAPING Preheat the oven to 180°C (350°F/gas 4). Cut the sausages of cookie dough into slices 5 mm–1 cm (¼–½ in) thick and arrange on a baking tray (pan) spaced well apart.

BAKING Bake for 8–10 minutes, depending on whether you like your cookies soft in the middle or cooked right through.

The idea is to bake the number of cookies you need at a time, so they can be eaten when still hot.

Week 03

Monday
Baked eggs with mushrooms

Tuesday
Roast autumn vegetables with mozzarella

Wednesday
Spaghetti with meatballs

Thursday
Cabbage, fennel and mozzarella pizza

Friday
Cabbage and split pea soup with meatballs

Special treat
Bread pudding

TIMING 🕐

2 H
IN THE
KITCHEN

**SEASON:
AUTUMN**

Out of season, substitute the grapes and squash with celeriac (celery root) and an apple.

VEGETARIAN

Substitute the meatballs with courgette (zucchini) fritters (week 11).

IF YOU DON'T LIKE

Cauliflower: substitute with broccoli.

For storing

1 container about 300 ml
(10 fl oz/1¼ cups)
2 containers about 750 ml
(25 fl oz/3 cups)
2 containers about 1.5 litres
(51 fl oz/6 cups)
1 tea (dish) towel

Utensils

2 oven dishes
1 casserole dish (Dutch oven), sauté
or frying pan (skillet)
1 large saucepan
1 baking tray (pan)
1 food processor
4 ramekins

WEDNESDAY

MONDAY

THURSDAY

FRIDAY

SPECIAL TREAT

TUESDAY

Fruit, vegetables and herbs

- ❏ 6 little gem lettuces
- ❏ 500 g (1 lb 2 oz) button mushrooms
- ❏ 1 bunch of flat-leaf parsley
- ❏ 1 bundle of chives
- ❏ 1 small green cabbage or small pointed cabbage
- ❏ 1 small cauliflower
- ❏ garlic cloves
- ❏ 4 onions
- ❏ 7 shallots
- ❏ 1 small butternut squash
- ❏ 1 bunch of grapes
- ❏ 1 lemon
- ❏ 1 apple

Chilled produce

- ❏ 500–600 g (1 lb 2 oz– 1 lb 5 oz) pizza dough or 2 ready-made pizza rounds
- ❏ 500 g (1 lb 2 oz) minced (ground) meat (beef and/or veal and/or pork)
- ❏ 200 ml (7 fl oz/scant 1 cup) crème fraîche
- ❏ 100 g (3½ oz) butter
- ❏ 15 eggs
- ❏ 500 g (1 lb 2 oz) mozzarella or burrata
- ❏ 1 litre (34 fl oz/4 cups) full-fat (whole) milk
- ❏ 60 g (2 oz) Parmesan

General groceries

- ❏ 500 g (1 lb 2 oz) spaghetti or linguine
- ❏ 500 ml (17 fl oz/2 cups) passata (sieved tomatoes)
- ❏ marmalade
- ❏ 2 × 400 g (14 oz) tins chopped tomatoes
- ❏ 2 organic vegetable or chicken stock cubes
- ❏ 120 g (4 oz/½ cup) split peas

Baked goods

- ❏ stale bread (about 1½ baguettes)

Storecupboard

- ❏ olive oil
- ❏ dried oregano or thyme
- ❏ caster (superfine) sugar
- ❏ fennel seeds
- ❏ mustard
- ❏ salt and pepper

1. Advance preparation

🕐 30 minutes

Clean the mushrooms and cut two-thirds of them into strips.
Wash and spin the salad leaves. → **TEA (DISH) TOWEL OR JAR** → **REFRIGERATOR**
Wash the parsley and chives and drain. De-stalk the parsley but keep the stalks to one side. Cut the hard part of the base and any damaged leaves from the cabbage and rinse. Take off around a dozen leaves and cut the heart into 4 to 5 pieces.
Rinse the cauliflower, remove any damaged leaves but keep the rest and quarter it. Wash the squash. Remove the seeds with a spoon and keep the skin. Cut the squash into 4 to 5 large pieces.
Rinse the grapes and apple.
Peel 7 garlic cloves, the onions and 3 shallots. Thinly slice the shallots.
Rinse the split peas.

2. Meatballs and tomato sauce

🕐 30 minutes

THE MEATBALLS Blend the parsley leaves in a food processor, remove half and set aside for other preparations. Blend 120 g (4 oz) stale bread for the breadcrumbs and ½ onion in a food processor. Grate (shred) 3 garlic cloves and 30 g (1 oz) Parmesan. Carefully mix these ingredients with the meat and an egg, a little salt and pepper (taste and check the seasoning). Form into balls the size of ping-pong balls. Brown in a frying pan (skillet) over a medium-high heat, then reduce the heat to cook through (do this in 2 batches so as not to crowd the frying pan). Allow to cool. → **CONTAINER** → **REFRIGERATOR**

THE TOMATO SAUCE Blend 2 onions in the food processor. In a casserole dish (Dutch oven), cook the blended onions with a pinch of salt. When they are tender and transparent, add 2 garlic cloves, the tinned tomatoes, 200 ml (7 fl oz/ scant 1 cup) passata (sieved tomatoes), some thyme or oregano, a pinch of salt and sugar and some pepper. Stir and simmer over a medium-low heat. Allow to cool. Blend if you would like a very smooth sauce. → **CONTAINER** → **REFRIGERATOR**

3. Vegetables and soup

🕐 10 minutes

THE VEGETABLES In an oven dish, combine the butternut squash, three-quarters of the cauliflower, 4 cabbage leaves, the grapes, 4 crushed but not peeled garlic cloves, 4 unpeeled shallots. Sprinkle with oregano, salt and pepper, then drizzle generously with olive oil. → **COVER WITH CLING FILM (PLASTIC WRAP)** → **REFRIGERATOR**

THE SOUP In a saucepan, put half the cabbage, the remaining cauliflower, the split peas, the quartered apple (no need to peel), 2 sprigs of oregano or thyme, the parsley stalks, 1½ onions, a garlic clove, the stock cubes and enough water to cover. Bring to a simmer and cook for 35 minutes then blend. Allow to cool. → **CONTAINER** → **FREEZER**

4. Pizza dough

🕐 5 minutes

THE PIZZA DOUGH Roll out the dough into a disc, place on a baking tray (pan) lined with baking parchment. → **COVER WITH CLING FILM (PLASTIC WRAP)** → **FREEZER**

5. Cabbage and mushroom condiment

🕐 15 minutes

THE CABBAGE Boil the salted water. Blanch 8 cabbage leaves for 2 minutes, then immerse in cold water. Drain.
→ TEA (DISH) TOWEL → REFRIGERATOR
THE MUSHROOM CONDIMENT Finely chop the remaining cabbage. Chop the chives and whole mushrooms together, add one-third of the finely sliced shallots, salt, 1 teaspoon finely grated lemon zest, 2 tablespoons lemon juice, 6 tablespoons olive oil (enough to fully cover the mixture) and pepper. Season the cabbage with 2 tablespoons of this mixture. **→ CONTAINER → REFRIGERATOR**
The rest of this condiment: **→ JAR → REFRIGERATOR**

6. Mushrooms for the baked eggs

🕐 15 minutes

Slice the remaining onion and brown them with the remaining thinly sliced shallots in 2 tablespoons olive oil. When golden, add 1 tablespoon chopped parsley, a garlic clove, then the crème fraîche. Season with salt and pepper and simmer gently for 5 minutes. Allow to cool. **→ CONTAINER → REFRIGERATOR**

7. Bread pudding

🕐 15 minutes

Slice the bread, butter it and spread with marmalade. Arrange the slices in a buttered oven dish. Beat the milk with 6 eggs and 50 g (2 oz/¼ cup) sugar; pour over the bread. **→ FILM → REFRIGERATOR**

Monday

Baked eggs with mushrooms

🕐 Ready in 15 minutes, including 5 minutes prep

THE COOKING Preheat the oven to 150°C (300°F/gas 1). Butter 4 ramekins (custard cups) and share out the sliced mushrooms for the baked eggs. Break 2 eggs into each ramekin. Place the ramekins in an oven dish. Half fill the dish with water to make a bain-marie and bake for 10–20 minutes, depending on how well done you like your eggs.

THE ACCOMPANIMENT Serve with a few lettuce leaves (keep some for Wednesday and Thursday), simply seasoned with lemon juice and olive oil, as well as some bread and butter.

Roast autumn vegetables with mozzarella

🕐 Ready in 1 hour, including 5 minutes prep

COOKING THE VEGETABLES Preheat the oven to 190°C (375°F/gas 5). Take the dish of vegetables and bunch of grapes out of the refrigerator (separate the bunch into 2–3 smaller bunches, but do not de-stalk). Drizzle generously with olive oil and bake for about 1 hour. The vegetables should be tender, nicely roasted and their skins beginning to brown in places.

THE MOZZARELLA Serve with half of the mozzarella (or burrata), garnished with the mushroom condiment (keep some for the Thursday salad and the Friday soup). The shallots are eaten by pressing the flesh out of the skin.

Wednesday

Spaghetti with meatballs

🕐 Ready in 20 minutes, including 5 minutes prep

THE PASTA Cook the spaghetti in a large quantity of boiling salted water for the time stated on the packet.
THE SAUCE AND MEATBALLS While the spaghetti is cooking, reheat the tomato sauce and meatballs together over a low heat. Keep 4–8 meatballs in their container for the soup, this time in the freezer! Drain the pasta, pour a little olive oil on top, stir, arrange onto plates and distribute the sauce.
THE SEASONING Sprinkle with parsley and grate (shred) Parmesan on top. Serve with lettuce leaves seasoned with a little lemon juice and olive oil.

Cabbage, fennel and mozzarella pizza

Ready in 20 minutes, including 10 minutes prep

THE PIZZA Preheat the oven to 220°C (430°F/gas 8). Take the dough out of the freezer. Spread on top
300 ml (10 fl oz/1¼ cups) passata (sieved tomatoes). Tear and lay out the blanched cabbage leaves, sprinkle with
½ teaspoon fennel seeds and lay out the remaining mozzarella (or burrata). Bake in the oven for 10 minutes.
THE ACCOMPANIMENT Serve with lettuce leaves seasoned with olive oil, lemon juice and a little mushroom
condiment (keep some for Friday).
FOR FRIDAY Put the soup and remaining meatballs into the refrigerator to defrost.

Cabbage and split pea soup with meatballs

🕐 Ready in 10 minutes, including 5 minutes prep

Reheat the soup over a medium-low heat and add the meatballs at the last minute.
Serve the soup with the rest of the mushroom condiment, 1 or 2 meatballs per bowl and some bread.

Bread pudding

🕐 Ready in 30–35 minutes

Preheat the oven to 190°C (375°F/gas 5) and bake the bread pudding for 30–35 minutes: it should be nice and golden. It can be eaten hot or cold.

Week 04

Monday
One-pot pasta with cauliflower, lemon, Cheddar and rosemary

Tuesday
Broccoli flans with salad

Wednesday
Cream of vegetable soup

Thursday
Vegetable curry with rice

Friday
Camembert and potatoes with salad

Special treat
Baked apples

TIMING 🕐

1 H 40
MINUTES IN
THE KITCHEN

**SEASON:
AUTUMN–
WINTER**
Out of season,
substitute the apples
for apricots.

**IF YOU DON'T
LIKE**
Broccoli: substitute
with spinach.

For storing
5 containers about 300 ml
(10 fl oz/1¼ cups)
2 containers about 750 ml
(25 fl oz/3 cups)
4 containers about 1.5 litres
(51 fl oz/6 cups)
3 tea (dish) towels

Utensils
1 steamer
1 medium saucepan
1 stock pot
8 ramekins
1 casserole dish (Dutch oven) or sauté pan
1 food processor
1 oven dish

Shopping

Fruit, vegetables and herbs

- ❏ 1 medium-sized cauliflower
- ❏ 6 carrots
- ❏ 4 leeks
- ❏ 2 cos (romaine) lettuces
- ❏ 1 bunch of small turnips (5–6 turnips)
- ❏ 1 onion
- ❏ 1 bunch of chervil
- ❏ 1 bunch of coriander (cilantro)
- ❏ 3–4 sprigs of rosemary
- ❏ 2 small heads of broccoli
- ❏ 1 pomegranate
- ❏ 1 lemon
- ❏ 3 cm (1¼ in) ginger root
- ❏ 12 apples
- ❏ 20 small potatoes

Chilled produce

- ❏ 1 litre (34 fl oz/4 cups) full-fat (whole) milk
- ❏ 250 g (9 oz) mild Cheddar or tomme
- ❏ 1 camembert or Vacherin Mont d'Or
- ❏ 40 g (1½ oz) butter
- ❏ 500 ml (17 fl oz/2 cups) thick crème fraîche
- ❏ 4 eggs

General groceries

- ❏ 300 g (10½ oz/1½ cups) long-grain rice
- ❏ 500 g (1 lb 2 oz) pasta (use wholemeal pasta if you prefer)
- ❏ 150 g (5 oz/1 cup) whole almonds
- ❏ 1 × 250 ml (8½ fl oz/1 cup) tin coconut milk

Storecupboard

- ❏ Indian spice mix: curry, garam masala
- ❏ white wine (optional)
- ❏ salt and pepper
- ❏ honey
- ❏ nutmeg
- ❏ olive oil

1. Advance preparation

🕐 30 minutes

Wash the broccoli and cauliflower. Cut the thick stalk off the broccoli and dice into 1–2 cm (½–¾ in) pieces. Divide the cauliflower and the rest of the broccoli into small florets. Peel the carrots. Cut 3 into 5 cm (2 in) sections, the other 3 into 1–2 cm (½–¾ in) dice. Clean the leeks: cut off the roots, remove any damaged leaves, cut off the hard end of the green part, split in half from the top downwards and rinse in a bowl of cold water. Drain. Cut 2 into 5 cm (2 in) sections and the other 2 into 1–2 cm (½–¾ in) strips. Scrub or peel the turnips (if they are young, there's no need to peel them). Cut half into 4–5 pieces, the rest into 1–2 cm (½–¾ in) dice. Peel 6 potatoes: cut 4 into sections and the other 2 into small dice. Scrub the remaining potatoes well and leave to dry.
Wash and spin the lettuce. ➔ **TEA (DISH) TOWEL** ➔ **REFRIGERATOR**
Rinse the rosemary. Cut off the leaves and chop finely.
Rinse the chervil and coriander (cilantro), then drain.
Cut the leaves off the coriander, keep the stalks (not any parts that are too hard) and chop them. Store the leaves. ➔ **JAR** ➔ **REFRIGERATOR**
Peel and thinly slice the onion. Grate the ginger finely.

2. For the pasta

🕐 15 minutes

Grate (shred) the Cheddar with a coarse grater. Store two-thirds in a container.
➔ **CONTAINER** ➔ **REFRIGERATOR**
Combine three-quarters of the cauliflower, the finely grated zest of half a lemon, half of the chopped rosemary, a little salt and pepper and 2 tablespoons olive oil.
➔ **CONTAINER** ➔ **REFRIGERATOR**

3. Flans and vinaigrette

🕐 20 minutes

THE FLANS Boil in salted water or steam three-quarters of the broccoli stems for 10 minutes. Blend in the food processor with half of the chervil and 1 tablespoon olive oil (store the rest of the chervil). ➔ **TEA (DISH) TOWEL** ➔ **REFRIGERATOR**.
Beat 4 eggs, 250 ml (8½ fl oz/1 cup) crème fraîche, 250 ml (8½ fl oz/1 cup) milk, salt and pepper; add the remaining Cheddar and a little freshly grated nutmeg. Mix with the puréed broccoli. ➔ **CONTAINER** ➔ **REFRIGERATOR**
THE VINAIGRETTE In a jar, mix the finely grated zest of half a lemon, 3 tablespoons lemon juice, 6 tablespoons olive oil, salt, pepper, then shake. ➔ **JAR** ➔ **REFRIGERATOR**

4. Soup

 10 minutes

Combine the small diced carrots, turnips, potatoes, broccoli base, strips of leek, remaining cauliflower and the other half of the chopped rosemary in a container. Drizzle with 1 tablespoon olive oil.
→ CONTAINER → FREEZER

5. Curry

 15 minutes

THE VEGETABLES AND SPICES
Grind 100 g (3½ oz/⅔ cup) almonds in the food processor with the coriander stalks. Heat 3 tablespoons oil in a casserole dish (Dutch oven). Brown the finely sliced onion for 5 minutes. Add the grated ginger and stir for 1 minute. Add 2 teaspoons spices and stir for 1 minute, then add the vegetables cut into sections (carrots, leeks, turnips, potatoes and the rest of the broccoli) and stir. Add the ground almonds, 100 ml (3½ fl oz/scant ½ cup) water and the coconut milk, then stir, cover and simmer for 30 minutes. Allow to cool.
→ CONTAINER → FREEZER
THE POMEGRANATE Cut the pomegranate into quarters. Open the inside of the fruit gently with your hands, then hold it over a bowl and tap the skin with a wooden spatula to release the seeds into the bowl. Finish shelling it with your hands. **→ JAR → REFRIGERATOR**

6. Apples

 10 minutes

Wash the apples well, remove the core with a corer or small knife. Drizzle with a little lemon juice. Push a small spoonful of honey and a knob of butter into each apple, sprinkle with a dash of freshly grated nutmeg. **→ COVER WITH CLING FILM (PLASTIC WRAP) OR USE A CONTAINER → REFRIGERATOR**
Roughly chop the remaining almonds.
→ JAR → CUPBOARD

One-pot pasta with cauliflower, lemon, Cheddar and rosemary

🕐 Ready in 20 minutes, including 5 minutes prep

Bring a large quantity of salted water to a boil. Add the pasta and herby cauliflower.
Cook for the time stated on the packet. Drain, add the cheese, stir and serve.

Broccoli flans with salad

🕐 Ready in 30 minutes, including 5 minutes prep

THE FLANS Preheat the oven to 150°C (300°F/gas 1). Butter 8 ramekins (custard cups)
(2 per person) or a large mould and pour in the broccoli mixture. Place the ramekins or
mould in an oven dish, half fill with water and bake for 30 minutes.
THE SALAD Season half of the lettuce with half of the vinaigrette. Serve with bread.

Cream of vegetable soup

🕐 Ready in 35 minutes, including 10 minutes prep

Provide bread to go with this dish. Heat 750 ml (25 fl oz/3 cups) water. When it begins to boil, add the small vegetable dice and simmer for 25 minutes. Blend with 750 ml (25 fl oz/3 cups) milk and add the chervil (keep a little aside for garnish). Serve with chervil leaves, a little cream and some bread.

FOR THURSDAY Put the curry in the refrigerator to defrost.

Vegetable curry with rice

🕐 Ready in 20 minutes, including 10 minutes prep

THE RICE Cook the rice: rinse, then put in a saucepan with 1.5 times its volume of water and 1 teaspoon salt. Bring to the boil, lower the heat immediately, tightly close with a lid and cook for 11 minutes. Remove the lid, stir gently with a fork and place a clean tea (dish) towel over the rice.

THE CURRY While the rice is cooking, reheat the curry. Serve with the rice, sprinkled with coriander leaves and half the pomegranate seeds.

Camembert and potatoes with salad

🕐 Ready in 40 minutes, including 10 minutes prep

THE MONT D'OR Preheat the oven to 223°C (450°F/gas 8). Open the box of camembert, make a hollow in the middle and pour in a small glass of white wine (optional). Bake for 25 minutes.

THE POTATOES Immerse the potatoes in cold water, add salt and cook for about 30 minutes. They should be soft when pricked with the tip of a knife. Drain.

THE SALAD Put the remaining lettuce leaves in a salad bowl, season with the remaining vinaigrette. Serve the melted cheese on the potatoes, and the salad as an accompaniment.

Baked apples

🕐 Ready in 40 minutes, including 5 minutes prep

Prepare on Monday or Tuesday. They will keep for several days.
Preheat the oven to 190°C (375°F/gas 5). Sprinkle the apples with chopped almonds
and bake for about 35 minutes: they should shrink considerably. Serve with cream and
the remaining pomegranate seeds.

Week 05

Monday
Poached chicken breasts, carrots and potatoes with pomegranate condiment

Tuesday
Onion and blue cheese puff pastry tart with watercress salad

Wednesday
Noodles with vegetables and chicken

Thursday
Fried eggs, onions and chilli with salad

Friday
Watercress soup

Special treat
Pancakes

TIMING 🕐

1 H 40
MINUTES IN THE KITCHEN

SEASON: AUTUMN–WINTER

Out of season, substitute watercress with baby spinach, rocket (arugula) or sorrel.

VEGETARIAN

Substitute the chicken dish with pistou soup (week 9) and the chicken in the noodle dish with some tofu.

IF YOU DON'T LIKE

Blue cheese: substitute with anchovies and olives or another type of cheese.

For storing
3 containers about 300 ml (10 fl oz/1¼ cups)
2 containers about 750 ml (25 fl oz/3 cups)
5 containers about 1.5 litres (51 fl oz/6 cups)
2 tea (dish) towels

Utensils
1 oven dish
1 baking tray (pan)
1 frying (skillet) or sauté pan
8 steamers
1 medium saucepan
1 large saucepan
1 hand-held blender

week 05 *Shopping*

Fruit, vegetables and herbs

- ❏ 2 bunches of watercress
- ❏ 10 carrots
- ❏ 300 g (10½ oz) mangetout (snow peas)
- ❏ 12 small potatoes
- ❏ 12 red onions
- ❏ 1 little gem or Batavia lettuce
- ❏ 1 celery heart
- ❏ 3 garlic cloves
- ❏ 3 shallots
- ❏ 3 fennel bulbs
- ❏ 1 lemon
- ❏ 1 pomegranate
- ❏ 1 bunch of fresh thyme
- ❏ 2 small chillies

Chilled produce

- ❏ 4 chicken breasts (700–800 g/ 1 lb 9 oz–1 lb 12 oz) in total)
- ❏ butter
- ❏ 150 g (5 oz) blue cheese
- ❏ 500 ml (17 fl oz/2 cups) full-fat (whole) milk
- ❏ 1 packet of puff pastry
- ❏ 12 eggs

General groceries

- ❏ 300 g (10½ oz) wheat noodles
- ❏ 21 g (¾ oz/7 teaspoons) baking powder
- ❏ 150 g (5 oz) green olives
- ❏ 5 organic chicken stock cubes

Storecupboard

- ❏ 400 g (14 oz/3¼ cups) plain (all-purpose) flour
- ❏ cider or wine vinegar
- ❏ caster (superfine) sugar
- ❏ olive oil
- ❏ soy sauce
- ❏ maple syrup
- ❏ salt and pepper

1. Chicken

🕐 5 minutes

Boil 1.5 litres (51 fl oz/6 cups) water, and dissolve 3 stock cubes into it. Pour this stock over the chicken breasts arranged in a wide saucepan (they should be completely covered) and place over a medium heat. Simmer for 5 minutes, then turn off the heat, cover and allow to cool. The chicken will poach in the liquid as it cools.
At the end of the cooking session, store the cooled chicken with its stock.
➔ **CONTAINER** ➔ **REFRIGERATOR**

2. Advance preparation

🕐 30 minutes

Peel the potatoes. Cut 8 into fat wedges and the rest into large cubes.
Peel the carrots. Cut 4 into fat wedges and 2 into large chunks.
Cut 4 carrots into fine sticks. Rinse the mangetout, then cut into fine sticks.
➔ **CONTAINER** ➔ **REFRIGERATOR**
Wash the fennel and cut into quarters or sixths.
Wash the watercress. Cut and discard the ends of any dirty, damaged stalks. Keep one bunch as it is. With the other bunch, remove the thicker stalks (set aside for the soup) and keep the leaves and fine stalks. ➔ **TEA (DISH) TOWEL**
➔ **REFRIGERATOR**
Wash and spin the lettuce. ➔ **TEA (DISH) TOWEL** ➔ **REFRIGERATOR**
Cut the pomegranate into quarters. Open the inside of the fruit with your hands, then hold it over a bowl and tap the skin with a wooden spoon to release the seeds into the bowl. Peel and thinly slice the onions and shallots. Peel the garlic and rinse the thyme. Rinse the celery.

3. Pomegranate condiment

🕐 15 minutes

Finely chop the celery and a small handful of watercress leaves.
Wash and thinly slice the chillies. Pit the olives and chop finely, mixing them with the chopped celery, watercress, shallots and a third of the chilli. Season with salt, add a little lemon juice and cover with olive oil. Add half of the pomegranate.
➔ **JAR OR CONTAINER** ➔ **REFRIGERATOR**

4. Onions, vegetables and tart

🕐 20 minutes

THE ONIONS Put the onions in a frying pan (skillet) with 4 tablespoons oil, a good pinch of salt and a pinch of sugar. Cook over a medium-gentle heat for 25 minutes: they should be cooked through and very lightly browned. Add the leaves of 2 sprigs of thyme.

THE VEGETABLES FOR THE CHICKEN While the onions are cooking, cut the carrots into thick wedges and boil in salted water (or steam). Five minutes before the end, add the fennel. Allow to cool, drizzle with a little olive oil. → **CONTAINER** → **REFRIGERATOR**

THE TART Roll out the pastry and lay it on a baking tray (pan). Cover with half of the onions, crumble the blue cheese on top and add a little more thyme. → **COVER WITH CLING FILM (PLASTIC WRAP)** → **REFRIGERATOR**

5. Pancake mixture

🕐 5 minutes

Sift together the flour and baking powder then mix with a large pinch of salt and 2 tablespoons sugar. → **JAR** → **CUPBOARD**

6. Sauce for the noodles

🕐 10 minutes

Mix half of the remaining chillies with 2 tablespoons soy sauce, 2 grated garlic cloves, 2 teaspoons sugar, the other half of the pomegranate seeds and 1 tablespoon lemon juice. Taste and adjust for acidity, saltiness and sweetness by adding lemon, sugar or soy sauce until you have a good balance. → **JAR** → **REFRIGERATOR**

7. Soup

🕐 15 minutes

Put one-third of the remaining onions into a saucepan, add the potatoes and carrots in large pieces, 2 ladlesful of poaching liquid from the chicken, 2 stock cubes and enough water to just cover the vegetables. Bring to a boil and cook for 20 minutes until the potatoes are tender. Add the newly washed watercress and the thick stalks from the other bunch. Cook for 5 minutes. Add a grated garlic clove. Blend (not too finely) or, preferably, pass through a food mill (not too fine a sieve/fine-mesh strainer). Allow to cool. → **CONTAINER** → **FREEZER** Store the remaining onions with the remaining chillies. → **CONTAINER** → **REFRIGERATOR**

Poached chicken breasts, carrots and potatoes with pomegranate condiment

🕐 Ready in 15 minutes, including 5 minutes prep

Remove the chicken from the stock. Reheat the stock gently with the accompanying vegetables, then cut the chicken into strips. Keep a quarter in the refrigerator for the noodles. Serve the stock with the chicken, vegetables and some pomegranate condiment on top (keep some for Tuesday and Friday).

Onion and blue cheese puff pastry tart with watercress salad

🕐 Ready in 35 minutes, including 5 minutes prep

Preheat the oven to 200°C (400°F/gas 6). Bake the tart for 25 minutes. Season the watercress leaves with a little lemon juice, salt, olive oil and some pomegranate condiment. Serve together.

Noodles with vegetables and chicken

🕐 Ready in 10 minutes

THE NOODLES Cook the noodles for 1 minute less than the time stated on the packet. Drain, rinse in cold water and drain again.

THE VEGETABLES Heat a little oil in a frying pan (skillet). Add the carrot sticks and mangetout (snow peas), stir for 3 minutes over a high heat, add the set-aside chicken, stir for 1 or 2 minutes, add the noodles and the sauce for the noodles, then stir-fry for 2 minutes. Serve.

Fried eggs, onions and chilli with salad

🕐 Ready in 15 minutes

THE EGGS Gently reheat the onions and chilli in a frying pan (skillet). Push to one side and break 4 eggs into the pan. When they are cooked, take them out and cook 4 more eggs (according to your appetite).

THE SALAD Season the salad with lemon juice, salt, olive oil and pepper. Serve with bread.

FOR FRIDAY Put the soup in the refrigerator to defrost.

Watercress soup

🕐 Ready in 10 minutes, including 5 minutes prep

Reheat the soup. Serve with bread and the rest of the pomegranate condiment.

Pancakes

🕐 Ready in 20 minutes

THE PANCAKE MIXTURE Beat 4 eggs and the milk together. Pour into the dry mixture. Stir but not too much: the mix can remain slightly lumpy.

THE COOKING Heat a frying pan (skillet) and grease it with some butter and a piece of kitchen towel. Pour three small ladlefuls of mixture to form 3 pancakes. When small bubbles form on the surface, turn over and cook for another minute. Lay the pancakes on a plate and cover with kitchen foil to keep warm. Butter the frying pan again and continue until you have used up all the mixture. Serve with maple syrup.

Week 06

SEASON:
LATE WINTER
In the spring, use
young seasonal
vegetables

Monday
Beef stew with persillade

Tuesday
Next-day beef stew salad

Wednesday
Risotto

Thursday
Noodles in beef stew stock with
lemongrass sauce

Friday
Croque monsieur with salad

Special treat
Shortbread biscuits

VEGETARIAN
Choose another
menu, but you can
still make the risotto
from this menu using
vegetable stock.

IF YOU DON'T
LIKE
Turnips: substitute
with more leeks.

For storing
6 containers about 300 ml
(10 fl oz/1¼ cups)
3 containers about 750 ml
(25 fl oz/3 cups)
2 containers about 1.5 litres
(51 fl oz/6 cups)
1 tea (dish) towel or freezer bag
cling film (plastic wrap)

Utensils
1 large stockpot
1 frying pan (skillet)
1 food processor
1 baking tray (pan) or mould

FRIDAY

THURSDAY

WEDNESDAY

TUESDAY

MONDAY

SPECIAL TREAT

Fruit, vegetables and herbs

- ❏ 1 leek
- ❏ 25 small potatoes
- ❏ 1 celery heart
- ❏ 10 carrots
- ❏ 1 small bunch of turnips
- ❏ 3 onions
- ❏ 1 bouquet garni (thyme, bay, flat-leaf parsley)
- ❏ 2 cos (romaine) lettuces
- ❏ 4 shallots
- ❏ 1 bunch of flat-leaf parsley
- ❏ 1 bunch of coriander (cilantro)
- ❏ 1 lemon
- ❏ 1 punnet cherry tomatoes or other seasonal salad vegetable
- ❏ 1 green cabbage or 1 small pointed cabbage
- ❏ 4 sticks of lemongrass

Chilled produce

- ❏ 2.5 kg (5 lb 10 oz) stewing beef (ideally a mixture of different cuts: shoulder, shin, best rib, etc. Ask your butcher for advice. You can also use marrowbone.)
- ❏ 8 slices boiled ham
- ❏ 400 g (14 oz) Comté
- ❏ 250 g (9 oz) butter, taken out of the refrigerator beforehand
- ❏ crème fraîche

General groceries

❑ 400 g (14 oz/1¾ cups) risotto rice

❑ 300 g (10½ oz) Chinese egg noodles (or soba noodles)

❑ large capers and/or gherkins (cornichons) and other pickled vegetables

❑ 2 organic vegetable stock cubes

❑ 2–3 saffron threads

Storecupboard

❑ cloves

❑ olive oil

❑ sunflower oil

❑ soy sauce

❑ crunchy peanut butter

❑ plain (all-purpose) flour

❑ white wine

❑ mustard

❑ caster (superfine) sugar

❑ black peppercorns

❑ salt and pepper

1. Advance preparation

🕐 30 minutes

Clean the leek by cutting off the roots and splitting it in two lengthways (start at the green end without going right to the bottom) then rinse in cold water. Then cut into sections.

Peel the carrots and cut them into sections if they are large.

Clean the turnips and cut into large quarters. Peel the onions and shallots. Chop 2 onions. Clean the potatoes and place in cold water.
→ CONTAINER → REFRIGERATOR

Wash and spin the salad leaves. **→ TEA (DISH) TOWEL OR FREEZER BAG → REFRIGERATOR**

Wash and drain the herbs, then snip off the leaves. Rinse the celery. Rinse the cabbage and cut into pieces.
→ TEA (DISH) TOWEL OR FREEZER BAG → REFRIGERATOR

2. Beef stew

🕐 15 minutes

THE MEAT AND VEGETABLES Put the meat, a third of the turnips and carrots, the leek and the celery into a large stewpot with cold water. Store all the other vegetables. **→ CONTAINER → REFRIGERATOR**

THE BOUQUET GARNI Add 10 peppercorns, an onion studded with 2 cloves and the bouquet garni. Bring to a boil, then lower the heat and simmer for 3–4 hours, skimming regularly. Allow to cool. Drain the meat and vegetables, keeping the stock. Store the stock. **→ CONTAINER → REFRIGERATOR**

Store the vegetables and meat. **→ CONTAINER → REFRIGERATOR**

3. Persillade and lemongrass sauce

🕐 10 minutes

PREPARATION Blend together or chop by hand 2 shallots with the parsley and coriander leaves, setting aside a few herbs. Divide this mixture in 2. **→ JAR → REFRIGERATOR**

THE PERSILLADE To half of this mixture, add a little salt and pepper, a dash of lemon, a little mustard and cover with olive oil. **→ JAR → REFRIGERATOR**

THE LEMONGRASS SAUCE Blend the other half of the mixture with the tender heart of 4 sticks of lemongrass, 2 tablespoons soy sauce and 2 teaspoons sugar. Add 2 tablespoons sunflower oil and 2 tablespoons peanut butter. **→ JAR → REFRIGERATOR**

4. Risotto

🕐 20 minutes

Grate (shred) 250 g (9 oz) Comté.
→ CONTAINER → REFRIGERATOR
Chop two shallots. In a saucepan,
sweat with 30 g (1 oz) butter and a
pinch of salt over a fairly low heat for
7–8 minutes: the shallots should become
transparent but not begin to colour.
→ CONTAINER → REFRIGERATOR

5. Croque monsieur

🕐 15 minutes

In 20 g (¾ oz) butter, sweat the 2 chopped onions with a pinch of salt
over a medium-low heat for 12–15 minutes: the onions should be tender and
slightly golden. Add a pinch of sugar and a dash of soy sauce. Allow to cool.
→ CONTAINER → REFRIGERATOR

6. Shortbread biscuits

🕐 30 minutes

Put 200 g (7 oz) butter in a large bowl,
work with a spatula until very soft, add
90 g (3¼ oz) sugar and a pinch of salt,
beat again. Add 300 g (10½ oz/
2½ cups) sifted flour and the finely
grated zest of the lemon. Mix to form
a dough without working for too long.
Spread by hand to a thickness of about
2 cm (¾ in) on a baking tray (pan) lined
with baking parchment or in a buttered
mould. Flatten the surface with a jar.
**→ COVER WITH CLING FILM (PLASTIC
WRAP) → REFRIGERATOR**

Beef stew with persillade

🕐 Ready in 25 minutes, including 10 minutes prep

THE VEGETABLES Discard the fat that has congealed on the surface of the stock. Bring to a boil. Immerse the potatoes in this. After 15 minutes, add the carrots, cabbage and turnips, then cook for 10–15 minutes.

THE MEAT Take out the vegetables, put the meat and vegetables that were cooked with the meat into the stock to reheat them. Set aside a third of the meat and freshly cooked vegetables. Keep almost all of the stock, except for 4 ladlefuls for serving.

SERVING Serve the meat and vegetables with a little stock, some persillade (keep some for Tuesday and Friday), mustard and gherkins.

Next-day beef stew salad

🕐 Ready in 20 minutes, including 10 minutes prep

Place half the salad leaves (keep the other half for Friday) in a bowl. Then, cube the remaining meat and arrange on top of the leaves. Add diced gherkins, halved cherry tomatoes, cold cooked vegetables and 150 g (5 oz) diced Comté. Season with the persillade (keep a little for Friday). Serve with bread.

Risotto

⏰ Ready in 25 minutes

THE STOCK Heat up almost all the remaining stock (keep back 2–3 ladlefuls). If necessary, thin with water and dissolved stock cubes to obtain about 1.2 litres (40 fl oz/4¾ cups). Add the saffron threads.

THE RICE Put the cooked shallots into a frying pan (skillet) or saucepan. When they are warmed through, add the rice and stir until coated. Add 120 ml (4 fl oz/½ cup) white wine, allow to evaporate over a medium-high heat. Add the stock, one ladle at a time, stirring until each ladleful is absorbed. After 20 minutes, the rice should be al dente. Add 2 tablespoons crème fraîche, half the grated (shredded) cheese and some chopped flat-leaf parsley. Stir and serve.

Noodles in beef stew stock with lemongrass sauce

🕐 Ready in 25 minutes, including 15 minutes prep

Cook the noodles according to the instructions on the packet (usually 4 minutes in boiling salted water). Drain and rinse in cold water. Reheat the remaining 2–3 ladlefuls of stock. Serve the noodles on a base of stock, with the lemongrass sauce and remaining herbs.

Croque monsieur with salad

🕐 Ready in 20 minutes, including 15 minutes prep

THE ONIONS AND BREAD Preheat the oven to 180°C (350°F/gas 4). In a frying pan (skillet) reheat the caramelised onions, then take them out. Brown the slices of bread in batches in the frying pan with a little butter (for a lighter version, toast them under the grill).

THE SANDWICHES Make sandwiches with the slices of ham cut to fit the bread, 2 slices in each sandwich, some grated (shredded) Comté and onions. Put in the oven for 5–10 minutes, but keep an eye on the cooking. Serve with the salad seasoned with the remaining persillade (or oil, lemon and salt).

Shortbread biscuits

🕐 Ready in 1 hour, including 5 minutes prep

Preheat the oven to 150°C (300°F/gas 1). With a knife, mark (without really cutting) the sections of the shortbread. Bake for 45 minutes–1 hour depending on the thickness: they should remain quite pale in colour. Allow to cool, then cut the biscuits along the marked lines.

Week 07

**SEASON:
SPRING**

Out of season,
substitute parsley
for the mint.

Monday

Chicken tikka kebabs with rocket

Tuesday

Goat's cheese and herb omelette
with rocket

Wednesday

Chicken biryani with cranberries

Thursday

Rice bowl, roast broccoli
and yoghurt dressing

Friday

Herb and ravioli soup

Special treat

Granola

VEGETARIAN

Substitute the
chicken kebabs
with a vegetable tart
(week 9) without
ham and leave the
chicken out of the
biryani.

**IF YOU DON'T
LIKE**

Broccoli: substitute
with asparagus when
in season.

For storing

3 containers about 300 ml
(10 fl oz/1¼ cups)
2 containers about 750 ml
(25 fl oz/3 cups)
2 containers about 1.5 litres
(51 fl oz/6 cups)
1 tea (dish) towel or freezer bag
cling film (plastic wrap)

Utensils

1 large oven dish
12 kebab skewers
1 baking tray (pan)
1 large saucepan
1 large frying pan (skillet)

FRIDAY

WEDNESDAY

THURSDAY

SPECIAL TREAT

TUESDAY

MONDAY

Fruit, vegetables and herbs

❑ 1 bunch of dill

❑ 1 bunch of coriander (cilantro)

❑ 300 g (10½ oz) rocket (arugula)

❑ 2 heads of broccoli

❑ 1 bunch of mint

❑ several sprigs of oregano or thyme, fresh or dried

❑ 1 orange

❑ fresh fruit of your choice

❑ 5 cm (2 in) ginger root

❑ 500 g (1 lb 2 oz) podded peas (can be frozen)

❑ 3 lemons

❑ 3 small red onions

❑ 1 bunch of flat-leaf parsley

❑ 4 garlic cloves

Chilled produce

❑ 5 chicken breasts or boneless chicken thighs

❑ 1 kg (2 lb 4 oz/4 cups) Greek-style yoghurt

❑ 12 eggs

❑ 200 g (7 oz) fresh goat's cheese

❑ 200 ml (7 fl oz/scant 1 cup) cream or coconut milk, whichever you prefer

❑ 60 g (2 oz) butter

❑ 2 packs of ravioli (about 500 g/1 lb 2 oz)

General groceries

- ❏ 500 g (1 lb 2 oz/2½ cups) basmati rice
- ❏ 2 tablespoons grated (shredded) coconut (optional)
- ❏ 125 g (4 oz/1 cup) hazelnuts
- ❏ 2 tablespoons seeds of your choice
- ❏ 200 g (7 oz) cranberries
- ❏ 8–12 pitta breads
- ❏ 300 g (10½ oz/2 cups) oat flakes

Storecupboard

- ❏ spice mix
- ❏ garam masala
- ❏ olive oil
- ❏ 4 organic vegetable stock cubes
- ❏ paprika
- ❏ honey
- ❏ dried oregano or thyme
- ❏ salt and pepper

1. Advance preparation

🕐 30 minutes

If you are using wooden skewers, soak them in water for 30 minutes. Next, wash the herbs. De-stalk the parsley, mint and coriander (cilantro).
→ JAR → REFRIGERATOR
Wash the broccoli, removing any damaged parts. Cut off and keep the stalk and separate the head into florets. Peel the onions, ginger (unless it's organic) and garlic. Slice an onion. **→ CONTAINER**
→ REFRIGERATOR
Mix the broccoli with a grated garlic clove, 1 teaspoon garam masala, a little thyme or oregano, salt and 2 tablespoons of olive oil.
→ CONTAINER → REFRIGERATOR
Wash the rocket (arugula) and spin gently. **→ TEA (DISH) TOWEL → REFRIGERATOR**

2. Yoghurt dressing

🕐 5 minutes

Mix 500 g (1 lb 2 oz/2 cups) yoghurt, the finely grated zest of a lemon, 3 tablespoons lemon juice, 2 tablespoons olive oil, 2 grated garlic cloves, a few snipped oregano or thyme leaves and salt. Taste and adjust for seasoning. Store half of this dressing. **→ CONTAINER → REFRIGERATOR**

3. Chicken marinade

🕐 10 minutes

THE MARINADE To the remaining yoghurt dressing, add half of the grated ginger, 1 tablespoon garam masala and 1 teaspoon paprika.
THE KEBABS Cut the chicken into 2–3 cm (½–¾ in) pieces. Thread onto the skewers, lay across an oven dish, then coat in the marinade. **→ COVER WITH CLING FILM (PLASTIC WRAP) → REFRIGERATOR**

4. Soup

🕐 15 minutes

In a large saucepan, put the broccoli stalks, 300 g (10½ oz) peas, 2 stock cubes and add 1 litre (34 fl oz/4 cups) water. Bring to a boil and cook for 20 minutes, until the broccoli is tender. Add 2 grated garlic cloves, half of the remaining grated ginger, half of the parsley and coriander (cilantro), 150 g (5 oz) rocket (arugula), almost all of the dill and 5–6 mint leaves. Cook for 3 minutes, then blend with the cream or coconut milk. Allow to cool. **→ JAR → FREEZER**

5. Biryani

🕐 15 minutes

Chop 2 onions. Sweat in 30 g (1 oz) butter and a pinch of salt over a fairly gentle heat in a frying pan (skillet) or saucepan for 8–10 minutes. Add one grated garlic clove, the remaining grated ginger, stir for 1 minute, then add 1 tablespoon garam masala and a third of the cranberries. Allow to cool.
→ CONTAINER → REFRIGERATOR

6. Granola

🕐 15 minutes

THE GRANOLA Preheat the oven to 150°C (300°F/gas 1). Put the oat flakes into a large oven dish or onto a baking tray (pan), add 2 tablespoons olive oil, 2 tablespoons honey, three-quarters of the hazelnuts, the seeds, 2 tablespoons coconut (optional), a little lemon and orange zest and a pinch of salt.
THE COOKING Make 2 trays if the first is too full. Cook for 30 minutes, stirring from time to time. Allow to cool. Add the remaining cranberries.
→ JAR → CUPBOARD

Chicken tikka kebabs with rocket

🕐 Ready in 30 minutes, including 10 minutes prep

THE KEBABS Preheat the oven grill. Take the kebabs out of the refrigerator and keep them on their dish with the skewers of the kebabs resting on the edges. Grill for 15–20 minutes, turning once or twice. Reheat the pitta breads, slightly dampened, in the bottom of the oven. Keep 2–3 kebabs for the biryani, allow to cool and store in the refrigerator.

TO SERVE Serve the pitta breads, the chicken with its cooking juices and some yoghurt dressing (keep some for Thursday) sprinkled with a little paprika, with the rocket (arugula) leaves (keep some for Tuesday), a few mint leaves, lemon quarters and the sliced onion.

Goat's cheese and herb omelette with rocket

🕐 Ready in 10 minutes

THE EGGS Tear 5–6 mint leaves. Crack 12 eggs into a bowl, season with salt and pepper and, without beating the eggs, break up the yolks with a fork. Heat 30 g (1 oz) butter in a large frying pan (skillet) over a high heat, and pour in the eggs.

THE COOKING When the edges begin to firm, tilt the frying pan towards you and push the eggs with a spatula so that the uncooked egg in the middle slides towards the surface of the pan. When the edges are set again, crumble the goat's cheese on top and sprinkle some mint on top. Fold the omelette. Lower the heat and finish cooking. Serve with rocket (arugula) leaves seasoned with olive oil and lemon.

Wednesday

Chicken biryani with cranberries

🕐 Ready in 20 minutes, including 10 minutes prep

Reheat the biryani mixture. Add the peas. Chop up the chicken leftover from Monday and add it to the mixture and stir. Add the rice and 125 ml (4¼ fl oz/½ cup) boiling water into which a stock cube has been dissolved. Bring to the boil, lower the heat, cover and cook for 11 minutes. Serve sprinkled with chopped coriander (cilantro) and parsley and 1 tablespoon yoghurt.

Keep between a third and a half of the rice for Thursday.

Rice bowl, roast broccoli and yoghurt dressing

🕐 Ready in 30 minutes, including 5 minutes prep

Preheat the oven to 200°C (400°F/gas 6). Spread the broccoli florets on a baking tray (pan) and roast for 20 minutes.
Serve the cold rice mixed with the broccoli, topped with yoghurt dressing. Sprinkle with the remaining chopped hazelnuts.
FOR FRIDAY Defrost the soup in the refrigerator.

Herb and ravioli soup

🕐 Ready in 10 minutes, including 5 minutes prep

Reheat the soup. Bring some water with a stock cube to the boil, then cook the ravioli for the time stated on the packet (usually 2–3 minutes).
Serve the soup in bowls with the ravioli and some chopped dill.

Granola

🕐 Ready in 5 minutes

Serve the granola for breakfast with yoghurt and fresh fruit.

Week 08

TIMING

1 H 30
MINUTES IN
THE KITCHEN

**SEASON:
SPRING**

Out of season,
substitute tomatoes
and white peaches
for the fennel
and orange.

Monday
Fish gratin with lettuce

Tuesday
Pasta, fennel, orange and cashew salad

Wednesday
Ham quiche with lettuce

Thursday
Pasta with garlic-infused oil,
cucumber salad and yoghurt dressing

Friday
Pea soup with garlic crostini

Special treat
Scones

VEGETARIAN

Substitute the fish
dish with a vegetable
gratin (weeks 2
and 10).

**IF YOU DON'T
LIKE**

Peas: substitute
with broccoli or
asparagus.

For storing

6 containers about 300 ml
(10 fl oz/1¼ cups)
2 containers about 750 ml
(25 fl oz/3 cups)
2 containers about 1.5 litres
(51 fl oz/6 cups)
1 tea (dish) towel or freezer bag
cling film (plastic wrap)

Utensils

2 oven dishes
1 large saucepan
1 hand-held blender
1 small saucepan
fine sieve (fine-mesh strainer) or mouli

TUESDAY

THURSDAY

FRIDAY

WEDNESDAY

MONDAY

SPECIAL TREAT

Fruit, vegetables and herbs

❏ 600 g (1 lb 5 oz) potatoes

❏ 2 oranges

❏ 1 lettuce of your choice

❏ 4 fennel bulbs

❏ 1 large cucumber
(or 2 small ones)

❏ 1 lemon

❏ 1 bunch of basil

❏ 7 garlic cloves

❏ 800 g (1 lb 12 oz) peas
(can be frozen)

Chilled produce

❏ 900 g (2 lb) fish fillets,
such as hake

❏ 1 packet of shortcrust pastry

❏ 300 g (10½ oz) feta

❏ 3 eggs

❏ 100 g (3½ oz) butter

❏ 200 ml (7 fl oz/scant 1 cup)
crème fraîche

❏ 750 g (1 lb 10 oz/3 cups)
Greek-style yoghurt

❏ 200 ml (7 fl oz/scant 1 cup)
full-fat (whole) milk

❏ 250 g (9 oz) cured ham
(smoked or unsmoked)

General groceries

- ❏ 1 kg (2 lb 4 oz) pasta
- ❏ 100 g (3½ oz/⅔ cup) cashews

Storecupboard

- ❏ olive oil
- ❏ 400 g (14 oz/3¼ cups) plain (all-purpose) flour
- ❏ 60 g (2 oz/¼ cup) caster (superfine) sugar
- ❏ 7 g (¼ oz) sachet baking powder
- ❏ honey or jam (jelly)
- ❏ nutmeg
- ❏ salt and pepper

Sunday

1. Advance preparation

🕐 25 minutes

Peel and rinse the potatoes. In a large saucepan, cover them with cold salted water, bring to the boil and cook for 10 minutes. Cut into thin slices. Wash and spin the lettuce. → **TEA (DISH) TOWEL OR FREEZER BAG** → **REFRIGERATOR**

Remove any damaged parts of the fennel, slice finely from top to bottom. Place half the slices in iced water. → **CONTAINER** → **REFRIGERATOR**

Peel the garlic cloves. Wash, drain and snip off the basil leaves.

3. Fish gratin

🕐 15 minutes

Preheat the oven to 180°C (350°F/gas 4). Drizzle a little garlic oil over the bottom of an oven dish. Cut the fish fillets into pieces and arrange them in the bottom of the dish. Add 100 g (3½ oz) peas, then the thin slices of potatoes in rows. Drizzle with a little oil. Bake for about 40 minutes until the fish and potatoes are tender. Allow to cool. → **COVER WITH CLING FILM (PLASTIC WRAP)** → **REFRIGERATOR**

2. Infused oil, yoghurt dressing and fennel

🕐 15 minutes

THE FENNEL Fry half the fennel slices for 5 minutes over a medium-high heat with 1 tablespoon olive oil. Season with salt and pepper. → **CONTAINER** → **REFRIGERATOR**

THE INFUSION Slice 6 garlic cloves. Put in a small saucepan with 300 ml (10 fl oz/1¼ cups) olive oil. Heat gently for 10 minutes. Turn off the heat and add around 10 basil leaves. Allow to cool, then strain (you can skip this if you like having pieces of garlic and leaves in the oil). → **JAR** → **REFRIGERATOR**

THE YOGHURT DRESSING Mix 300 g (10½ oz/1¼ cups) yoghurt with a grated garlic clove, a little lemon zest, 2 teaspoons lemon juice and salt. → **JAR** → **REFRIGERATOR**

4. Soup

 10 minutes

Put 700 g (1 lb 9 oz) peas and 1 tablespoon infused oil into a saucepan. Heat for 5 minutes over a medium heat, stirring, then add enough water to just cover the peas and cook for 10 minutes. Add half of the remaining basil, 150 g (5 oz/⅔ cup) yoghurt and blend or, preferably, pass through a fine sieve (fine-mesh strainer) or a mouli (this is best for getting rid of small skins). Allow to cool. **→ JAR → FREEZER**

Store the rest of the basil. **→ CONTAINER → REFRIGERATOR**

5. Pasta

 10 minutes

Boil 400 g (14 oz) pasta for the time stated on the packet. Drain, drizzle with olive oil and allow to cool.

→ CONTAINER → REFRIGERATOR

6. Quiche

 10 minutes

Beat together 3 eggs, 200 ml (7 fl oz/scant 1 cup) cream and 300 g (10½ oz/1¼ cups) yoghurt. Season with salt, pepper and freshly grated nutmeg.

→ CONTAINER → REFRIGERATOR

7. Vinaigrette

 5 minutes

In a jar, mix 2 tablespoons lemon juice, 1 tablespoon orange juice, a little lemon zest, 1 tablespoon infused oil and 5 tablespoons plain olive oil. Season with salt and pepper, then shake.

→ JAR → REFRIGERATOR

8. Scones

 20 minutes

THE DOUGH Mix the flour, baking powder and sugar, add a pinch of salt, 1 teaspoon finely grated zests of orange and lemon. Add the butter, cut into pieces, and rub into the flour with your fingertips. Add the milk and fold in gently to bind the dough.

FORMING THE SCONES Flatten the dough by hand until about 2.5 cm (2 in) thick and cut into discs with a cookie cutter or a floured glass. Lay on a baking tray (pan). **→ COVER WITH CLING FILM (PLASTIC WRAP) → FREEZER**

Once the scones are frozen, it is possible to remove them from the tray and store in a container or freezer bag to save space.

Fish gratin with lettuce

🕐 Ready in 25 minutes, including 5 minutes prep

Preheat the oven to 170°C (340°F/gas 3). Reheat the fish gratin for 20 minutes.
Serve with lettuce (keep some for Wednesday) dressed with vinaigrette.

Pasta, fennel, orange and cashew salad

🕐 Ready in 10 minutes

THE SALAD If possible, take the pasta out of the refrigerator in advance. Mix with the cashews, then the drained raw fennel and the fried fennel.

THE ORANGE Peel and remove the inner membrane from the orange and slice.

THE SEASONING Mix with the other ingredients and season with yoghurt dressing and vinaigrette.

Ham quiche with lettuce

🕐 Ready in 40 minutes, including 10 minutes prep

Preheat the oven to 180°C (350°F/gas 4). Line a baking tin with pastry. Prick with a fork.
Cut 150 g (5 oz) ham into strips and lay them on the pastry. Pour the quiche mixture on top
and bake for 30–35 minutes. Serve with the lettuce seasoned with vinaigrette.

Pasta with garlic-infused oil, cucumber salad and yoghurt dressing

🕐 Ready in 20 minutes, including 10 minutes prep

Cook the pasta. Peel and thinly slice the cucumbers, and mix with the yoghurt dressing. Drain the pasta and season with the infused oil. Sprinkle with basil.

FOR FRIDAY Defrost the soup in the refrigerator.

Pea soup with garlic crostini

(⏱) Ready in 20 minutes, including 10 minutes prep

Reheat the soup over a gentle heat. Slice and toast the bread (under the grill or in a toaster), drizzle with infused oil and lay the remaining slices of ham, some feta and basil on top.

Scones

⏱ Ready in 15 minutes, including 5 minutes prep

Defrost as many scones as you would like to eat on a baking tray (pan) for at least 20 minutes (or the night before, for breakfast). Preheat the oven to 180°C (350°F/gas 4). Bake the scones 12–15 minutes, depending on their size. Serve with butter and honey or jam.

Week 09

Monday
Hake, green beans and radishes
with pesto and bulgur

Tuesday
Swiss chard tarts with cherry tomatoes

Wednesday
Pasta with pesto

Thursday
Vegetable couscous with merguez

Friday
Pistou soup

Special treat
Baked rhubarb

VEGETARIAN

Substitute the fish
dish with a shakshuka
(week 10) and leave
out the meat in the
tart and soup.

**SEASON:
SPRING**

Out of season,
substitute green
cabbage for the
green beans.

**IF YOU DON'T
LIKE**

Swiss chard:
substitute with
leeks or courgettes
(zucchini).

For storing
4 containers about 300 ml
(10 fl oz/1¼ cups)
2 containers about 750 ml
(25 fl oz/3 cups)
3 containers about 1.5 litres
(51 fl oz/6 cups)
cling film (plastic wrap)

Utensils
2 large saucepans
1 frying pan (skillet)
1 food processor
1 oven dish

FRIDAY

THURSDAY

WEDNESDAY

SPECIAL TREAT

MONDAY

TUESDAY

Shopping

Fruit, vegetables and herbs

- ❏ 1 kg (2 lb 4 oz) young green beans
- ❏ 1 bundle of baby carrots
- ❏ 1 bunch of radishes
- ❏ 3 large courgettes (zucchini)
- ❏ 4 small bundles of Swiss chard (about 1 kg/2 lb 4 oz)
- ❏ 2 oranges
- ❏ 1 lemon
- ❏ 1 bundle of young turnips
- ❏ 1 fennel bulb
- ❏ 6 garlic cloves
- ❏ 3–4 cm (1¼–1½ in) ginger root
- ❏ 2 punnets of cherry tomatoes
- ❏ 3 onions
- ❏ 3 bunches of basil
- ❏ 1 kg (2 lb 4 oz) rhubarb

Chilled produce

- ❏ 150–200 g (5–7 oz) smoked ham
- ❏ 400 g (14 oz) Comté or tomme
- ❏ hake: fillets or whole fish gutted and scaled (about 600 g/1 lb 5 oz) if fillets or 1.2 kg/2 lb 10 oz) if whole fish)
- ❏ 500 ml (17 fl oz/2 cups) crème fraîche
- ❏ 8 merguez (spiced lamb sausages)
- ❏ 2 packets of puff pastry
- ❏ fresh goat's cheese
- ❏ 2 eggs

General groceries

- ❑ 60 g (2 oz) pumpkin seeds
- ❑ 500 g (1 lb 2 oz/2¾ cups) coarse bulgur or pre-seasoned couscous
- ❑ 1 × 400 g (14 oz) jar passata (sieved tomatoes)
- ❑ 500 g (1 lb 2 oz) pasta (such as spaghetti)
- ❑ 1 × 400 g (14 oz) tin chickpeas (garbanzos)

Storecupboard

- ❑ olive oil
- ❑ ras el hanout (a North African spice mix)
- ❑ 3 organic vegetable or chicken stock cubes
- ❑ a few threads of saffron (optional)
- ❑ 150 g (5 oz/¾ cup) caster (superfine) sugar
- ❑ salt and pepper

Sunday

1. Advance preparation

⏲ 30 minutes

Boil salted water in a large saucepan. Rinse and de-stalk the green beans. Immerse them in the boiling water for 5–8 minutes and remove them with a slotted spoon. Immerse in cold water. Allow to cool. → **JAR** → **REFRIGERATOR**

Rinse and dry the basil, then snip off the leaves. Store a few of the leaves.
→ **JAR** → **REFRIGERATOR**

Scrub the radishes and rinse (keep any healthy tops). Store half of them.
→ **JAR** → **REFRIGERATOR**

Clean the Swiss chard, separate the stalks from the leaves, then cut into strips. Immerse the stalks in boiling salted water. After 2 minutes, add the leaves, cook for 2 minutes and drain. Peel and dice the carrots. Clean and dice the turnips, fennel and courgettes (zucchini). Peel the garlic and ginger. Peel and thinly slice the onions.

2. Pesto

⏲ 10 minutes

THE PUMPKIN SEEDS Heat a dry frying pan (skillet) with no added oil over a medium heat. Toss in the pumpkin seeds and shake the pan to toast without burning them. As soon as they begin to split and turn brown, tip onto a plate.

PREPARATION Roughly blend the garlic leaves, radish tops and 1 tablespoon Swiss chard with 100 ml (3½ fl oz/ scant ½ cup) olive oil, 2 garlic cloves, grated, half the pumpkin seeds, salt and pepper. Put in a jar and cover with oil.
→ **JAR** → **REFRIGERATOR**

Keep the rest of the seeds in a jar.
→ **JAR** → **CUPBOARD**

3. Vegetables for the couscous and soup

⏲ 20 minutes

Put 3 tablespoons olive oil into a large saucepan and sweat the onions for 7–8 minutes over a medium-low heat. Pour half into another saucepan.

THE COUSCOUS VEGETABLES In the first saucepan, add the grated ginger and 2 grated garlic cloves, stir for 1 minute, then add 2 teaspoons ras el hanout and stir for 1 minute. Add half of the carrots, turnips and radishes, then stir well. Add almost the whole jar of passata and half of the chickpeas, 2 stock cubes and enough water to cover the vegetables. Then add 2–3 pieces of orange peel cut with a vegetable peeler. Bring to a simmer, add the saffron, cover and cook for 25 minutes. Add a third of the courgettes (zucchini) and cook for a further 10 minutes. Allow to cool. → **CONTAINER** → **FREEZER**

THE SOUP In the other saucepan, add the carrots, turnips and half of the fennel, stirring well each time. Then add half of the remaining courgettes and cover with water. Add a stock cube and season with salt and pepper. Simmer gently for 20 minutes, then add a quarter of the Swiss chard. Allow to cool. → **CONTAINER** → **FREEZER**

4. Tarts

 10 minutes

Preheat the oven to 180°C (350°F/gas 4). Roll out the pastry. Arrange the Swiss chard on top, season with salt and pepper, add slices of ham, torn or cut, then grate (shred) 300 g (10½ oz) Comté on top. Beat together 2 eggs with 300 ml (10 fl oz/1¼ cups) cream and season with salt and pepper and a grated garlic clove, then pour over the tart. Bake for about 25 minutes. Allow to cool. **→ COVER WITH CLING FILM (PLASTIC WRAP) → FREEZER**

5. Hummus

 10 minutes

THE HUMMUS Blend the remaining chickpeas with 2 tablespoons olive oil, salt, pepper, a little finely grated lemon zest, 2 teaspoons lemon juice, a grated garlic clove and a few basil leaves.
→ JAR → FREEZER

6. Bulgur and fish

15 minutes

THE BULGUR Pour over the bulgur twice its volume of boiling salted water. Add 2 tablespoons olive oil. Allow to swell for 10 minutes. Or follow the instructions on the packet if different, slightly reducing the cooking time. Allow to cool. Divide into 2 containers. **→ CONTAINER → REFRIGERATOR** or **→ CONTAINER → FREEZER**
THE FISH Season the fish with olive oil, the lemon zest and zest from an orange (we will add the juice on Monday), salt, pepper and basil. Add the remaining courgettes (zucchini), the fennel and remaining tomatoes. **→ CONTAINER → REFRIGERATOR**

7. Rhubarb

15 minutes

Rinse the rhubarb well, cut off any damaged edges, then cut the stalks into sections. Put in an oven dish with the sugar, zest of ½ orange and 2 tablespoons orange juice.
→ COVER WITH CLING FILM (PLASTIC WRAP) → REFRIGERATOR

Hake, green beans and radishes with pesto and bulgur

Ready in 30–50 minutes, including 10 minutes prep

THE FISH AND BULGUR Take the bulgur out of the refrigerator. Preheat the oven to 120°C (250°F/gas 1). Put the fish and its vegetables into an oven dish, then add some lemon and orange juice. Bake for 20 minutes if you have fillets, 30 minutes for a whole fish of 400–500 g (14 oz–1 lb 2 oz) or 40–50 minutes for a whole fish of 1 kg (2 lb 4 oz) or more.

THE VEGETABLES Put the green beans in a dish, season with a quarter of the pesto and some lemon juice. Thinly slice the radishes and sprinkle over the beans. Add pumpkin seeds and torn basil leaves. Serve the fish with the green beans and bulgur.

FOR TUESDAY Defrost the Swiss chard tarts in the refrigerator.

Swiss chard tarts with cherry tomatoes

🕐 Ready in 20 minutes, including 10 minutes prep

Preheat the oven to 160°C (320°F/gas 2) and reheat the Swiss chard tarts for 15 minutes. Meanwhile, cut the cherry tomatoes in half and season with a dash of olive oil. Serve the tarts with the tomato salad.

Pasta with pesto

🕐 Ready in 15 minutes, including 5 minutes prep

Cook the pasta in a large quantity of boiling salted water. Grate (shred) the rest of the Comté. Mix the pasta with two-thirds of the remaining pesto and the Comté. Season well with pepper and serve.

FOR THURSDAY Defrost the vegetable couscous and bulgur in the refrigerator.

Vegetable couscous with merguez

🕐 Ready in 25 minutes, including 10 minutes prep

Preheat the oven to 220°C (430°F/gas 8). Reheat the vegetable couscous. Put the merguez into an oven dish and cook for 15–20 minutes towards the top of the oven. Reheat the bulgur with one or two ladlefuls of vegetable stock. Serve.

FOR FRIDAY Defrost the soup and the hummus in the refrigerator.

Pistou soup

🕐 Ready in 10 minutes, including 5 minutes prep

Reheat the soup, stir in 2–3 tablespoons hummus. Serve with goat's cheese, slices of ham, pesto, hummus and bread.

Baked rhubarb

Ready in 20 minutes, including 5 minutes prep

Preheat the oven to 180°C (350°F/gas 4). Cover the dish of rhubarb with aluminium foil and bake for 20 minutes. Serve with crème fraîche, soft white cheese or yoghurt.

Week 10

TIMING ⏰

1 H 45
MINUTES IN
THE KITCHEN

SEASON:
SUMMER

Monday
Chicken tabbouleh

Tuesday
Gazpacho and hummus

Wednesday
Green shakshuka with feta

Thursday
Summer vegetable pasta

Friday
Gratin with sardines

Special treat
Raspberry clafoutis

VEGETARIAN
Substitute the
chicken with tofu
and the sardines
with soft-boiled eggs.

IF YOU DON'T
LIKE
Feta: substitute with
mozzarella.

For storing

4 containers about 300 ml
(10 fl oz/1¼ cups)
4 containers about 750 ml
(25 fl oz/3 cups)
2 containers about 1.5 litres
(51 fl oz/6 cups)
cling film (plastic wrap)

Utensils

1 baking tray (pan)
2 oven dishes
1 food processor
1 frying pan (skillet)

MONDAY

WEDNESDAY

TUESDAY

THURSDAY

FRIDAY

SPECIAL TREAT

Fruit, vegetables and herbs

- ❏ 8–10 courgettes (zucchini)
- ❏ 20 ripe tomatoes
- ❏ 2 cucumbers
- ❏ 3 red (bell) peppers
- ❏ 5 garlic cloves
- ❏ 2 bunches of flat-leaf parsley
- ❏ 2 lemons
- ❏ 1 bunch of spring onions (scallions) (7 onions)
- ❏ 2 bunches of mint
- ❏ 300 g (10½ oz) raspberries (can be frozen)
- ❏ 1 bunch of basil
- ❏ 1 bunch of coriander (cilantro)
- ❏ 200 g (7 oz) podded peas (can be frozen)

Chilled produce

- ❏ 150 g (5 oz) feta
- ❏ 400 ml (13 fl oz/ generous 1½ cups) full-fat (whole) milk
- ❏ 16 eggs
- ❏ 10 g (½ oz) butter
- ❏ 2–3 chicken breasts
- ❏ 400 ml (13 fl oz/generous 1½ cups) crème fraîche
- ❏ 40 g (1½ oz) Parmesan

General groceries

❏ 1 x 400 g (14 oz) tin chickpeas (garbanzos)

❏ Grand Marnier or Cointreau (optional)

❏ 150 g (5 oz/scant 1 cup) bulgur

❏ 100 g (3½ oz) pitted olives

❏ tinned sardines (enough for 4 people, according to appetite)

❏ 500 g (1 lb 2 oz) pasta

❏ 150 g (5 oz/1 cup) whole almonds

Storecupboard

❏ olive oil

❏ 75 g (2½ oz/scant ¾ cup) plain (all-purpose) flour

❏ cumin seeds

❏ 75 g (2½ oz/⅓ cup) caster (superfine) sugar

❏ salt and pepper

❏ coriander seeds

Sunday

1. Advance preparation

⏱ 20 minutes

Rinse and snip the herb leaves. **→ JAR →
REFRIGERATOR**
Wash all the vegetables. Slice the
tomatoes.
Cut 5 or 6 courgettes (zucchini):
into 5 mm (¼ in) slices. Dice the rest.
Cut two-thirds of the cucumbers into
large pieces, one-third into small dice.
Cut two-thirds of the (bell) peppers
into large pieces, one-third into dice.
Peel the garlic and onions. Thinly slice
4 onions. Store 2 of them chopped
with the small diced cucumber, add
1 tablespoon lemon juice, 3 tablespoons
olive oil, salt and pepper. **→ CONTAINER
→ REFRIGERATOR**

2. Dukkah

⏱ 10 minutes

In a frying pan (skillet) heated dry over
a medium heat, toast the almonds.
Take out half, then add 2 tablespoons
coriander seeds and 1 tablespoon
cumin. Coarsely grind this mixture and
season with salt and pepper. This is
dukkah. **→ JAR → CUPBOARD**
Grind the rest of the almonds for longer
until finely ground.

3. Bulgur and chicken

⏱ 15 minutes

THE BULGUR Pour over the bulgur twice
its volume of boiling salted water. Add
2 tablespoons olive oil. Allow to swell
for 10 minutes. Or follow the instructions
on the packet if different, slightly reducing
the cooking time. Allow to cool.
→ CONTAINER → REFRIGERATOR.
THE CHICKEN Cut the chicken into
strips. Brown in the oil over a high heat,
add 1 rounded teaspoon of cumin, lower
the heat to finish the cooking. Remove
from the heat and allow to cool.
→ CONTAINER → REFRIGERATOR

4. Gratin

⏱ 20 minutes

Preheat the oven to 180°C (350°F/gas 4). Rub an oven dish with half a garlic clove.
Alternate in the dish half of the tomato slices and two-thirds of the courgette
(zucchini) slices, adding the chopped onions and interspersing with one-third of the
basil leaves. Drizzle with olive oil. In another oven dish, or baking tray (pan), arrange
side by side the diced courgettes, diced (bell) peppers, half the remaining tomatoes
and the remaining courgette slices. Drizzle with oil, season with salt and pepper.
Cook both dishes for 40 minutes until everything is cooked through. Allow to cool.
Store the gratin. **→ COVER WITH CLING FILM (PLASTIC WRAP) → FREEZER**

5. Hummus

🕐 10 minutes

THE CHICKPEAS Blend half the chickpeas (garbanzos) with 2 teaspoons lemon juice and the zest of 1 lemon, 1 tablespoon ground almonds, 2 tablespoons olive oil, salt and pepper, 2 tablespoons fresh coriander (cilantro) and a grated garlic clove. Taste and adjust for seasoning. ➜ **CONTAINER** ➜ **REFRIGERATOR**
Put the rest of the chickpeas into the container with the cucumbers and onions. ➜ **CONTAINER** ➜ **REFRIGERATOR**

6. Gazpacho

🕐 5 minutes

THE GAZPACHO Put together half of the chilled roast tomatoes, slices of raw tomatoes, raw (bell) peppers, pieces of cucumber, half of the remaining basil, 2 tablespoons parsley, 2 grated garlic cloves, 3 onions, salt, pepper and 3 tablespoons olive oil. ➜ **CONTAINER** ➜ **REFRIGERATOR**

7. Pasta and green shakshuka

🕐 10 minutes

THE VEGETABLES FOR THE PASTA Chop the olives. Store them together with the roast vegetables: (bell) peppers, two-thirds of the diced courgettes (zucchini) and the remaining tomatoes. ➜ **CONTAINER** ➜ **REFRIGERATOR**
THE GREEN SHAKSHUKA Blend the slices of roast courgette with the remaining basil leaves. Store with the remaining diced courgette and add 2 tablespoons fresh coriander, 1 tablespoon parsley, the feta cut into cubes and the peas. ➜ **CONTAINER** ➜ **REFRIGERATOR**

8. Raspberry clafoutis

🕐 15 minutes

Set the oven to 200°C (400°F/gas 6). Butter an oven dish. Spread out the raspberries, sprinkle with a little sugar and drizzle with 2 tablespoons Grand Marnier. Whisk together the cream, milk, 8 eggs, 2 tablespoons ground almonds, the flour and the sugar. Pour over the fruit. Bake for 30–40 minutes. Allow to cool. ➜ **COVER WITH CLING FILM (PLASTIC WRAP)** ➜ **REFRIGERATOR**
Eat within 2 to 3 days.

Chicken tabbouleh

🕐 Ready in 10 minutes

THE HERBS Chop the remaining mint, parsley, coriander (cilantro) together.
THE VEGETABLES-CHICKEN-BULGUR MIXTURE Mix them with the cooked bulgur, add the seasoned cucumber-onion-chickpeas (garbanzos) mixture and the chicken.
Check the seasoning, sprinkle with a little dukkah, then serve.

Gazpacho and hummus

⏱ Ready in 10 minutes

Toast the bread and rub with the garlic. Blend the gazpacho mixture. Serve with the bread and hummus and sprinkle with dukkah.

Green shakshuka with feta

🕐 Ready in 15 minutes, including 10 minutes prep

THE SHAKSHUKA Pour the shakshuka mixture into a frying pan (skillet) with 2 tablespoons oil.
THE EGGS As soon as it is hot and is beginning to brown, break in 8 eggs, pushing aside the mixture to allow the egg white to cook through. Serve with bread.

Summer vegetable pasta

Ready in 15 minutes, including 5 minutes prep

Cook the pasta. Meanwhile, use a peeler to shave off Parmesan strips. Gently reheat the vegetable mixture and mix with the cooked pasta. Serve with the strips of Parmesan.

FOR FRIDAY Defrost the gratin in the refrigerator.

Gratin with sardines

Ready in 20 minutes, including 5 minutes prep

Reheat the gratin in the oven at 160°C (320°F/gas 2) (you can also eat this cold if you prefer).
Serve with the sardines and bread.

Raspberry clafoutis

🕐 Already made

Eat within 2 or 3 days.

Week 11

**SEASON:
SUMMER**

Out of season,
substitute mango for
the strawberries.

Monday
Rice bowl, courgette fritters and
aubergine-yoghurt dressing

Tuesday
Focaccia with lettuce

Wednesday
Vegetable lasagne

Thursday
Fried rice, saffron and apricots
with tomato salad

Friday
Red shakshuka

Special treat
Milkshake

**IF YOU DON'T
LIKE**

(Bell) peppers:
substitute with
additional slices of
aubergine (eggplant).

For storing
5 containers about 300 ml
(10 fl oz/1¼ cups)
5 containers about 750 ml
(25 fl oz/3 cups)
1 tea (dish) towel or freezer bag
cling film (plastic wrap)

Utensils
2 or 3 baking trays (pans)
1 oven dish
1 frying pan (skillet)
1 sauté pan or casserole dish (Dutch oven)
(or high-sided frying pan)

THURSDAY

SPECIAL TREAT

MONDAY

FRIDAY

WEDNESDAY

TUESDAY

Shopping

Fruit, vegetables and herbs

- ❏ 4 aubergines (eggplants)
- ❏ 30 ripe tomatoes
- ❏ 2 lettuces
- ❏ 300 g (10½ oz) baby rocket (arugula)
- ❏ 6 courgettes (zucchini)
- ❏ 5 onions
- ❏ 1 bunch of basil
- ❏ 2 red (bell) peppers
- ❏ rosemary
- ❏ 1 bunch of flat-leaf parsley
- ❏ 500 g (1 lb 2 oz) strawberries
- ❏ 2 lemons
- ❏ 7 garlic cloves

Chilled produce

- ❏ 500 g (1 lb 2 oz) mozzarella
- ❏ 60 g (2 oz) Parmesan
- ❏ 50 g (2 oz) feta
- ❏ 800 g (1 lb 12 oz/3¼ cups) Greek-style yoghurt
- ❏ 13 eggs
- ❏ ham or other cured meats
- ❏ 250 ml (8½ fl oz/1 cup) vanilla ice cream

General groceries

- ❏ 15 g (½ oz) fresh baker's yeast or 1 sachet (about 7 g/ ¼ oz) dried yeast
- ❏ 600 g (1 lb 5 oz/3¼ cups) long-grain white rice
- ❏ 500 g (1 lb 2 oz) lasagne sheets
- ❏ 4 tablespoons dried breadcrumbs
- ❏ pinch of saffron threads
- ❏ 50 g (2 oz) dried apricots
- ❏ 80 g (3 oz) cashews or hazelnuts (toasted if possible)

Storecupboard

- ❏ olive oil
- ❏ 500 g (1 lb 2 oz/4 cups) plain (all-purpose) flour
- ❏ smoked chilli or paprika
- ❏ salt and pepper
- ❏ oregano or thyme

1. Focaccia dough

🕐 15 minutes

Dissolve the yeast in 100 ml (3½ fl oz/ scant ½ cup) tepid water. Wait for 5 minutes. In a large bowl, mix the flour and 1 teaspoon salt. Make a well in the middle. Pour in the yeast, 200 g (7 oz/ ¾ cup) yoghurt, 4 tablespoons olive oil and 200 ml (7 fl oz/scant 1 cup) tepid water. Work into a dough (add a little flour or warm water if necessary) and knead in the food processor or by hand for 10 minutes. Cover the bowl and leave to rise for 2 hours.

2. Advance preparation

🕐 30 minutes

Rinse the aubergines (eggplants). Cut two into slices 3–4 mm (⅛ in) thick. In a large bowl, mix with 5 tablespoons olive oil, 2 teaspoons oregano or thyme, salt and pepper. Set out on baking trays (pans) in a single layer.

Rinse the tomatoes. Keep aside 10 and grate (shred) the rest with a coarse grater (this enables you to collect the flesh and remove part of the skin without having to peel them).

Wash the lettuces and rocket (arugula) ➜ **TEA (DISH) TOWEL OR FREEZER BAG** ➜ **REFRIGERATOR**

Rinse the (bell) peppers, remove the seeds and white membranes and slice thinly. Peel the onions and slice thinly. Peel the garlic.

Wash the courgettes (zucchini). Cut 3 of them into slices 3–4 mm (⅛ in) thick lengthways, set out on a baking tray (pan) and drizzle with a little olive oil. Grate the other 3 with a coarse grater.

Wash the herbs and snip off the leaves. Chop the parsley. Store a quarter of the basil. ➜ **CONTAINER** ➜ **REFRIGERATOR**

Rinse a sprig of rosemary, snip off the leaves and chop.

Chop the cashews. ➜ **CONTAINER** ➜ **CUPBOARD**

Chop the dried apricots.

3. Sauces

🕐 20 minutes

THE GARLIC AND ONIONS In a sauté pan, sweat the onions with 3 tablespoons olive oil and a pinch of salt over a medium-low heat for 7–8 minutes. Add 4 grated garlic cloves and stir. Set aside one-third.

THE TOMATOES AND PEPPERS Add the grated (shredded) tomatoes to the sauté pan. Add a pinch of sugar, 10 basil leaves and some pepper. Simmer for 30 minutes over a medium-low heat. Separately, brown the peppers for 5 minutes over a medium-low heat with 1 tablespoon olive oil. Add half of the tomato sauce and a large pinch (or more, according to taste) of smoked chilli or paprika. This is the sauce for the red shakshuka. Allow to cool. ➜ **CONTAINER** ➜ **FREEZER**

THE APRICOTS Take the onions you have set aside, add the chopped apricots and one spoonful of chopped parsley.
➜ **CONTAINER** ➜ **REFRIGERATOR**

4. Vegetables and lasagne

🕐 10 minutes

THE AUBERGINES AND COURGETTES Preheat the oven to 200°C (400°F/gas 6). Roast the trays of aubergines (eggplants) and courgettes (zucchini) for 15–20 minutes (swap levels in the oven twice). The courgettes will cook a little more quickly than the aubergines, so take them out first. Roast the 2 uncut aubergines for about 30 minutes. Keep 5 slices of courgette and 5 slices of aubergine for the focaccia. ➜ **CONTAINER**
➜ **REFRIGERATOR**

THE LASAGNE Rub an oven dish with a garlic clove cut in half. Make layers of courgette, aubergine, tomato sauce (the remaining half) and lasagne, interspersed with basil leaves and rocket as well as a layer of mozzarella (use 250 g/9 oz). Finish with a layer of breadcrumbs mixed with 1 tablespoon olive oil and 1 tablespoon parsley. Bake the lasagne for 25 minutes at 180°C (350°F/gas 4). Allow to cool. ➜ **COVER WITH CLING FILM (PLASTIC WRAP)**
➜ **FREEZER**

5. Courgettes, rice and aubergine sauce

🕐 10 minutes

THE COURGETTES Mix the grated (shredded) courgettes (zucchini) with 2 tablespoons chopped parsley, 5–6 torn basil leaves, 50 g (2 oz) crumbled feta, a handful of rocket (arugula), 5 eggs and 60 g (2 oz) grated Parmesan. Season.
➜ **CONTAINER** ➜ **REFRIGERATOR**

THE RICE Cook the rice in 1.5 times its volume of water. When it boils, sprinkle with saffron, stir, lower the heat, close tightly with a lid and cook for 11 minutes for it to absorb all the water. Season with olive oil, a little salt and pepper, and a dash of lemon. Divide in 2. ➜ **CONTAINERS** ➜ **REFRIGERATOR**

THE AUBERGINE SAUCE Crush the cooked whole aubergines (eggplants) with a fork and mix with a pinch of smoked chilli or paprika, a grated garlic clove, 1 tablespoon chopped parsley, 300 g (10½ oz/1¼ cups) yoghurt, some zest and a little lemon juice, salt and pepper. ➜ **CONTAINER** ➜ **REFRIGERATOR**

6. Focaccia

🕐 5 minutes

Push down the dough that has risen. Divide it in half. Spread each half into a rectangle, not too thin, make holes with your fingertips, drizzle with olive oil and place on baking trays (pans). ➜ **COVER WITH CLING FILM (PLASTIC WRAP)**
➜ **FREEZER**

7. Strawberries

🕐 5 minutes

Rinse and de-stem the strawberries, cut in half and mix with 300 g (10½ oz/ 1¼ cups) yoghurt. ➜ **CONTAINER**
➜ **REFRIGERATOR**

Rice bowl, courgette fritters and aubergine-yoghurt dressing

Ready in 25 minutes, including 10 minutes prep

THE RICE Take out one container of rice in advance if possible.

THE FRITTERS Heat 5 mm (¼ in) olive oil in a frying pan (skillet). Fry spoonfuls of grated (shredded) courgette (zucchini) mixture for 2–3 minutes on each side. Drain on paper towel.

Serve the rice and fritters with the aubergine-yoghurt dressing (keep half of this for Thursday), sprinkle with cashews (keep half of them for Thursday).

FOR TUESDAY Take out the trays of dough and put in the refrigerator.

Focaccia with lettuce

🕐 Ready in 20 minutes, including 10 minutes prep

Preheat the oven to 220°C (430°F/gas 8). Decorate the dough with slices of courgette (zucchini) and aubergine (eggplant), the remaining mozzarella, sea salt and chopped rosemary. Bake for 10–15 minutes. Serve with lettuce and cold cuts.

FOR WEDNESDAY Defrost the lasagne in the refrigerator.

Vegetable lasagne

Ready in 30 minutes, including 10 minutes prep

Reheat the lasagne in the oven at 180°C (350°F/gas 4). Serve with the lettuce, seasoned with a little salt, pepper, lemon and olive oil.

Fried rice, saffron and apricots with tomato salad

🕐 Ready in 15 minutes, including 10 minutes prep

THE RICE AND APRICOTS Take out the remaining rice and onion-apricot mixture. Heat the latter in a frying pan (skillet) over a high heat with 1 tablespoon of olive oil. Add the rice and sauté for 1–2 minutes until slightly golden.

THE ACCOMPANIMENT Sprinkle with cashews. Serve with the aubergine-yoghurt dressing.
Cut the remaining tomatoes and drizzle with a little salt and olive oil.

FOR FRIDAY Defrost the pepper sauce in the refrigerator.

Red shakshuka

🕐 Ready in 15 minutes, including 10 minutes prep

Reheat the shakshuka sauce in a frying pan (skillet). Break 8 eggs into the mixture. Cook over a medium heat until the whites are nicely set. Serve with some bread, slices of cold cuts and a rocket salad.

Milkshake

🕐 Ready in 5 minutes

Blend the strawberries with the yoghurt and vanilla ice cream, and a few basil leaves if you like.
Serve straight away.

Week 12

Monday
Salade Niçoise

Tuesday
Stuffed vegetables

Wednesday
Olive and goat's cheese pasta with buttered radishes

Thursday
Avocado and fried rice

Friday
Sage ravioli with cucumber

Special treat
Roasted fruit

TIMING 🕐
1 H 30
MINUTES IN THE KITCHEN

SEASON: SUMMER
Out of season, substitute the tomatoes and courgettes (zucchini) with onions.

VEGETARIAN
Substitute the sausage meat with chopped courgette (zucchini), herbs and onions.

IF YOU DON'T LIKE
Ravioli: substitute with potato gnocchi.

For storing
4 containers about 300 ml
(10 fl oz/1¼ cups)
4 containers about 750 ml
(25 fl oz/3 cups)
3 containers about 1.5 litres
(51 fl oz/6 cups)
1 tea (dish) towel or freezer bag
cling film (plastic wrap)

Utensils
2 oven dishes
1 stock pot
1 large frying (skillet) or sauté pan
1 food processor or blender

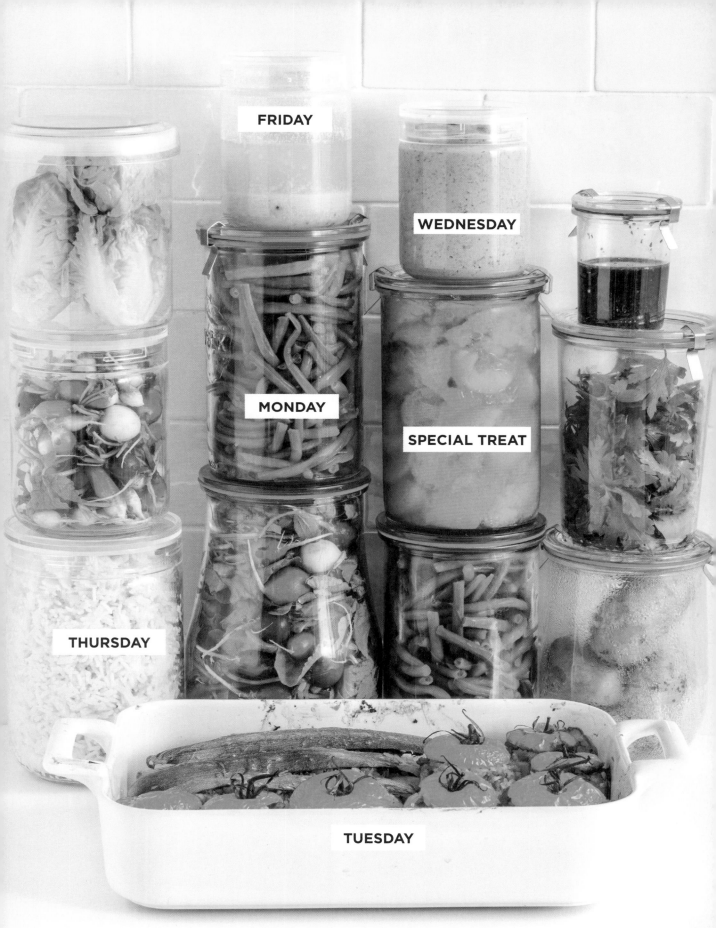

Shopping

Fruit, vegetables and herbs

- ❏ 1 kg (2 lb 4 oz) fine green beans
- ❏ 5–6 little gem lettuces (or other crisp lettuces)
- ❏ 8 courgettes (zucchini)
- ❏ 500 g (1 lb 2 oz) cherry tomatoes
- ❏ 8 large tomatoes
- ❏ 1 bunch of spring onions (scallions)
- ❏ 500 g (1 lb 2 oz) new potatoes
- ❏ 1 bunch of sage
- ❏ 2 bunches of radishes
- ❏ 2 avocados
- ❏ 2 large cucumbers (or 4 smaller ones)
- ❏ 1 lemon
- ❏ 1 bunch of basil
- ❏ 1 bunch of flat-leaf parsley
- ❏ a few sprigs of thyme
- ❏ 11 garlic cloves
- ❏ 150 g (5 oz) peas (can be frozen)
- ❏ 2 kg (4 lb 8 oz) mixture of peaches, plums and apricots
- ❏ 2 cm (¾ in) ginger root
- ❏ 1 red onion

Chilled produce

- ❑ 10 eggs
- ❑ crème fraîche
- ❑ 800 g (1 lb 12 oz) fresh ravioli
- ❑ 60 g (2 oz) butter
- ❑ 200 g (7 oz) fresh goat's cheese
- ❑ 500 g (1 lb 2 oz) sausage meat

General groceries

- ❑ 2 × 145 g (15 oz) tins line-caught tuna
- ❑ 100 g (3½ oz/⅔ cup) black olives
- ❑ 500 g (1 lb 2 oz) spaghetti
- ❑ 450 g (1 lb/2¼ cups) long-grain rice

Storecupboard

- ❑ olive oil
- ❑ soy sauce
- ❑ mustard
- ❑ caster (superfine) sugar
- ❑ salt and pepper

1. Cleaning

🕐 30 minutes

Wash the vegetables. Slice a cap off the top of the tomatoes and courgettes (zucchini). Using a teaspoon, scoop out and keep the flesh. For the large tomatoes, discard the seeds and keep the pulp.
Rinse the cherry tomatoes.
→ CONTAINER → REFRIGERATOR
Clean the onions and remove any dirty or damaged parts. Peel and thinly slice the red onion. Rinse, dry and snip off the leaves of the basil and flat-leaf parsley. Chop half and store the rest.
→ CONTAINER → REFRIGERATOR
Pit and chop the olives.
Wash all the fruit, de-stone and cut into quarters. Put in an oven dish.
Strip the thyme leaves off the stalks. Peel the garlic cloves. Wash and dry the lettuces.
→ TEA (DISH) TOWEL OR FREEZER BAG → REFRIGERATOR

2. Preparation of the vegetables

🕐 10 minutes

Wash the green beans. Steam or boil in salted water for 5 minutes. Cool in iced water, then drain. Chop a third of them. Store the chopped and whole beans separately. **→ CONTAINER → REFRIGERATOR** Clean the radishes.
Rinse and scrub the new potatoes, then steam or boil in salted water for 20 minutes (adjust the cooking time according to size) and allow to cool. **→ CONTAINER → REFRIGERATOR**

3. Stuffed vegetables

🕐 20 minutes

THE STUFFING In a large frying (skillet) or sauté pan, lightly brown the red onion in 2 tablespoons olive oil, over a medium heat. Add the sausage meat, stir to brown lightly and cook evenly. Add the flesh of the courgette (zucchini) and the tomato pulp, 50 g (2 oz/¼ cup) rice, the chopped basil and flat-leaf parsley. Season with salt and pepper, add the thyme, 4 grated garlic cloves, stir well and simmer gently for 15 minutes.
THE STUFFED VEGETABLES Preheat the oven to 180°C (350°F/gas 4). Stuff the scooped-out tomatoes and courgettes. Put on their caps and roast in the oven for 30–40 minutes. Allow to cool. **→ COVER WITH CLING FILM (PLASTIC WRAP) → REFRIGERATOR**

4. Fruit

🕐 10 minutes

Sprinkle the fruit with 1–2 tablespoons sugar and add lemon peel. Roast in the oven for 35–40 minutes at 180°C (350°F/gas 4). Allow to cool. ➜ **CONTAINER** ➜ **REFRIGERATOR**

5. Sauces and dressings

🕐 10 minutes

THE VINAIGRETTE Put a grated garlic clove, a pinch of finely grated lemon zest, 1 teaspoon mustard, 3 tablespoons lemon juice and 9 tablespoons olive oil in a jar and shake.

THE SAUCE FOR THE PASTA Blend half the remaining parsley, the goat's cheese and olives, 2–3 spring onions (scallions), add 1 tablespoon olive oil and a little salt. ➜ **CONTAINER** ➜ **REFRIGERATOR**

6. Rice and sauce

🕐 10 minutes

THE RICE Cook the remaining rice. Allow to cool.
➜ **CONTAINER** ➜ **REFRIGERATOR**
THE SAUCE FOR THE RICE Grate 2 cm (¾ in) ginger and 6 garlic cloves. Mix with a pinch of sugar, a dash of lemon juice and 4 tablespoons soy sauce. This is the sauce for the rice.
➜ **CONTAINER** ➜ **REFRIGERATOR**

Salade Niçoise

🕐 Ready in 20 minutes, including 10 minutes prep

THE VEGETABLES In a large dish, arrange the lettuce leaves, beans, potatoes and half the radishes, quartered (keep half for Wednesday), the cherry tomatoes, halved, slices of cucumber (keep some cucumber for Friday) and thin slices of spring onion (scallions).

THE TUNA AND EGGS Arrange the drained tuna and sprinkle torn basil leaves on top.
Boil 8 eggs for 3–4 minutes after reaching boiling point. Shell and halve them and add to the salad.
Drizzle with vinaigrette (keep some for Tuesday, Thursday and Friday). Serve with bread.

Stuffed vegetables

🕐 Ready in 30 minutes, including 5 minutes prep

Reheat the stuffed vegetables. Serve with lettuce leaves drizzled with vinaigrette.

Olive and goat's cheese pasta with buttered radishes

🕐 Ready in 15 minutes, including 5 minutes prep

Cook the pasta in boiling salted water. While the pasta is cooking, serve the radishes with butter and salt as an hors d'oeuvre. Once cooked, mix the pasta with the goat's cheese and olive sauce to serve.

Avocado and fried rice

🕐 Ready in 15 minutes, including 5 minutes prep

THE FRIED RICE Heat the oil in a large frying pan (skillet) over a high heat. Break 2 eggs into it and cook for 1 minute, stirring. Add the chopped green beans and peas, then stir. Add the rice, cook for about 2 minutes, then pour on the sauce for the rice, stir, then sprinkle with basil to serve.

THE AVOCADOS Serve the halved avocados with the vinaigrette as an hors d'oeuvre.

Sage ravioli with cucumber

🕐 Ready in 15 minutes, including 5 minutes prep

THE CUCUMBER Slice the cucumber. Add 1 teaspoon of crème fraîche to a little vinaigrette and drizzle over the cucumber. Sprinkle with chopped parsley or basil.

THE RAVIOLI In a frying pan (skillet), heat the butter over a low heat with 5–6 sage leaves.
Wait until the butter turns a slight hazelnut colour. Cook the ravioli (follow the instructions on the packet – it is usually very quick). Serve coated with sage butter.

Roasted fruit

Ready in 5 minutes

Serve the fruit with crème fraîche.

Week 13

Monday
Roast chicken, vegetables and tortilla wraps

Tuesday
Omelette with buttered radishes

Wednesday
Fried rice with chicken

Thursday
Red lentil and coconut milk soup
with tuna parcels

Friday
Carbonara

Special treat
Pear brownies

TIMING 🕐

1 H 40
MINUTES IN
THE KITCHEN

**SEASON:
SPRING–
SUMMER**

At the end of the
season, substitute
the radishes with
tomatoes.

VEGETARIAN

Substitute the
chicken with more
roast vegetables;
the tuna with more
fresh cheese; and
the lardons with
smoked tofu. Leave
the chicken out of
the rice.

**IF YOU DON'T
LIKE**

Pears: substitute with
walnuts.

For storing
2 containers about 300 ml
(10 fl oz/1¼ cups)
5 containers about 750 ml
(25 fl oz/3 cups)
5 containers about 1.5 litres
(51 fl oz/6 cups)
1 tea (dish) towel or freezer bag
cling film (plastic wrap)

Utensils
2 baking trays (pans)
1 stock pot
1 hand-held blender
1 cake tin

THURSDAY

TUESDAY

WEDNESDAY

MONDAY

SPECIAL TREAT

Fruit, vegetables and herbs

- ❏ 20 medium-sized tomatoes
- ❏ 1 bunch of radishes
- ❏ 2 avocados
- ❏ 6 courgettes (zucchini)
- ❏ 2 bunches of spring onions (scallions)
- ❏ 1 bunch of coriander (cilantro) leaves
- ❏ 12 garlic cloves
- ❏ 2 limes
- ❏ 4 cm (1½ in) ginger root
- ❏ a few sprigs of thyme

Chilled produce

- ❏ 6 chickens (drumsticks and thigh pieces)
- ❏ 20 eggs
- ❏ 1 packet of filo pastry
- ❏ 50 g (2 oz) Parmesan
- ❏ 300 g (10½ oz) fromage frais
- ❏ 300 g (10½ oz) butter
- ❏ 150 g (5 oz) pancetta or lardons

General groceries

- ❑ 300 g (10½ oz/1¾ cups) ready-spiced fine bulgur
- ❑ 300 g (10½ oz/1¼ cups) red lentils
- ❑ 250 ml (8½ fl oz/1 cup) coconut milk
- ❑ 12 tortilla wraps (or more, or less, depending on appetite)
- ❑ 300 g (10½ oz/1⅔ cups) rice
- ❑ 2 × 145 g (5 oz) tins line-caught tuna in oil
- ❑ 200 g (7 oz) chocolate
- ❑ 400 g (14 oz) pears in syrup
- ❑ 500 g (1 lb 2 oz) pasta

Storecupboard

- ❑ olive oil
- ❑ soy sauce
- ❑ cumin seeds
- ❑ smoked chilli
- ❑ 6 cardamom pods
- ❑ 1 cinnamon stick
- ❑ 130 g (1 oz/1 cup) plain (all-purpose) flour
- ❑ 225 g (8 oz/1 cup) caster (superfine) sugar
- ❑ salt and pepper

1. Advance preparation

🕐 20 minutes

Rinse, drain and snip the leaves off the coriander. ➜ **CONTAINER** ➜ **REFRIGERATOR**
Wash and halve the tomatoes. Wash the courgettes (zucchini), cut 4 into segments and 2 into rounds. Store the rounds.
➜ **CONTAINER** ➜ **REFRIGERATOR**
Clean the radishes. ➜ **CONTAINER** ➜ **REFRIGERATOR**
Clean and peel the onions.

2. Tray of chicken

🕐 20 minutes

THE BULGUR Put the bulgur in a bowl and cover it in the same volume of water.
➜ **CONTAINER** ➜ **REFRIGERATOR**
THE CHICKEN Preheat the oven to 180°C (350°F/gas 4). Halve the chicken thighs and lay them on a baking tray (pan). Intersperse with around 10 halved tomatoes and the segments of courgette (zucchini), without covering the chicken. Make another tray if there is not enough room. Sprinkle with smoked chilli, a little cumin and thyme, add 6 unpeeled and crushed garlic cloves and 6 onions. Drizzle with olive oil and coat well. Season with salt and pepper. Bake in the oven for 1 hour. Allow to cool. Set aside 2 chicken thighs. Store the rest. ➜ **COVER WITH CLING FILM (PLASTIC WRAP)** ➜ **REFRIGERATOR**

3. Salsa and soup

🕐 10 minutes

THE SOUP Rinse the lentils and put them in a saucepan with 4 tomatoes, 4 onions, 2 grated garlic cloves, 1 cm (½ in) grated ginger, 1 cinnamon stick, the cardamom pods and 1 teaspoon cumin. Cover with 300 ml (10 fl oz/1¼ cups) water. Cook for 20 minutes. Take out the cinnamon stick, 3 cardamom pods and blend until smooth. Allow to cool.
➜ **CONTAINER** ➜ **FREEZER**
THE SALSA Dice the remaining tomatoes, add 2 chopped onions and a handful of chopped coriander leaves. Season with salt, drizzle with a dash of lime juice and a little olive oil, then add a little smoked chilli. ➜ **CONTAINER** ➜ **REFRIGERATOR**

4. Fried rice with chicken

🕐 10 minutes

THE RICE Cook the rice and allow to cool. ➔ **CONTAINER** ➔ **REFRIGERATOR**
THE CHICKEN SKIN Skin the 2 set aside chicken thighs and chop.
THE SEASONING Grate 2 cm (¾ in) ginger and 4 garlic cloves. Mix with a pinch of sugar, a dash of lime juice, 4 tablespoons soy sauce and the cooked chicken. ➔ **CONTAINER** ➔ **REFRIGERATOR**

5. Tuna triangles

🕐 25 minutes

THE TUNA Drain the tuna. Mix with 200 g (7 oz) fromage frais, a third of the already chopped coriander and 1 cm (½ in) grated ginger.
THE FILO PARCELS Cut the filo pastry sheets in two. Brush half with olive oil, fold in half lengthways, put a little tuna stuffing at the end and fold to form a triangle. Use scissors to cut off any excess pastry at the end and place in a baking dish. Continue with the remaining sheets and stuffing. ➔ **COVER WITH CLING FILM (PLASTIC WRAP) OR USE A CONTAINER** ➔ **FREEZER**

6. Brownies

🕐 15 minutes

Butter a rectangular cake tin. Melt 250 g (9 oz) chocolate in a bain-marie with 200 g (7 oz) cubed butter. Add 225 g (8 oz/1 cup) sugar and 4 eggs, one by one, then the flour, very gently. Pour a little mixture into the baking tin, arrange the pears, then pour in the rest of the mixture. ➔ **COVER WITH CLING FILM (PLASTIC WRAP)** ➔ **REFRIGERATOR**

Roast chicken, vegetables and tortilla wraps

🕐 Ready in 20 minutes, including 10 minutes prep

THE CHICKEN AND TORTILLA WRAPS If possible, take out the chicken and bulgur in advance. Preheat the oven to 180°C (350°F/gas 4). Reheat the chicken for 20 minutes. Heat the slightly dampened tortilla wraps at the same time.

THE GUACAMOLE Halve the avocados, remove the stones, scoop out the flesh and crush with a fork with a little lime juice, salt, pepper and coriander.

Serve the chicken with the tortilla wraps, the guacamole, bulgur and the tomato salsa.

Omelette with buttered radishes

🕐 Ready in 10 minutes, including 5 minutes prep

Break 12 eggs into a large bowl, stir with a fork (no need to beat them, just enough to break the yolks and keep a fairly uneven texture). Season. Melt 25 g (¾ oz) butter in a frying pan (skillet) over a high heat. When the butter begins to foam, pour in the eggs. When they begin to go firm at the edges, push with a spatula, tilting the frying pan so that the uncooked mixture flows to the surface of the frying pan. Add the remaining fromage frais and a few flakes of Parmesan. Cook the way you like it, then fold. Serve with the radishes, butter and bread.

Fried rice with chicken

Ready in 10 minutes

Heat 1 tablespoon oil in a frying pan (skillet) and sauté the courgettes (zucchini), cut into rounds, for 2 minutes.
Add the rice and stir. Add the prepared chicken and stir. Serve sprinkled with coriander.
FOR THURSDAY Defrost the soup and the filo triangles in the refrigerator.

Red lentil and coconut milk soup with tuna parcels

🕐 Ready in 30 minutes, including 5 minutes prep

Preheat the oven to 180°C (350°F/gas 4). Cook the parcels for 25–30 minutes. Reheat the soup over a low heat. Add the coconut milk and some lime juice. Serve.

Carbonara

🕐 Ready in 20 minutes, including 10 minutes prep

THE PASTA Start cooking the pasta in boiling salted water.

THE CHEESY EGGS Separate the whites from the yolks of 4 eggs. Keep the whites for another recipe (can be frozen). Mix the yolks with the freshly-grated Parmesan. Brown the pancetta, cut into strips and add to the egg mixture.

THE SEASONING When the pasta is cooked, drain, keeping 1–2 tablespoons cooking water. Pour the pasta into the mixture with 1 tablespoon of water and stir to create a creamy sauce (add more water if needed). Serve with Parmesan.

Pear brownies

🕐 Ready in 20–30 minutes, including 2 minutes prep

Preheat the oven to 180°C (350°F/gas 4). Cook the brownie batter for 20–30 minutes. The cooking time depends on the size of the baking tin and thickness of the cake, whether you like it well cooked or very soft. Cut into squares. It will keep for 3–4 days in the refrigerator, but you can freeze part of it (and double the quantities if you want more!).

Create your own batch!

So how about making up your own menus?

To give you a hand, the following pages contain the shopping lists for each recipe's ingredients, so you can make up any combinations you want and devise your own week's menu. The labels at the end of the book will help you make your own labels for jars and containers.

Salads

Caesar salad (week 1)

FRUIT, VEGETABLES AND HERBS
- ❏ ⅓ large lettuce
- ❏ 1 garlic clove
- ❏ ½ lemon (2 teaspoons lemon juice)
- ❏ handful of flat-leaf parsley

CHILLED PRODUCE
- ❏ 4–8 eggs + 1 egg for the dressing
- ❏ 30 g (1 oz) Parmesan

GENERAL GROCERIES
- ❏ 2 anchovy fillets in oil + a few + 1 tablespoon oil from the anchovies
- ❏ 1 teaspoon mustard
- ❏ 150 ml (5 fl oz/scant ⅔ cup) olive oil
- ❏ pepper

Big broccoli and lentil salad with peanut dressing (week 2)

FRUIT, VEGETABLES AND HERBS
- ❏ 2 broccoli heads (florets only)
- ❏ 2 carrots
- ❏ 1 garlic clove
- ❏ 1 bunch of coriander (cilantro)
- ❏ 1 stick of lemongrass
- ❏ a few mint leaves

GENERAL GROCERIES
- ❏ 150 g (5 oz/¾ cup) green lentils
- ❏ 50 g (2 oz/⅓ cup) whole hazelnuts
- ❏ olive oil

PEANUT BUTTER DRESSING
- ❏ 1 chilli
- ❏ 2 shallots
- ❏ 1 stick of lemongrass
- ❏ 3 cm (1¼ in) ginger root
- ❏ 1 garlic clove
- ❏ 120 ml (4 fl oz/½ cup) cider vinegar
- ❏ 120 ml (4 fl oz/½ cup) soy sauce
- ❏ 3 tablespoons caster (superfine) sugar
- ❏ 2 tablespoons peanut butter

Next-day beef stew salad (week 6)

FRUIT, VEGETABLES AND HERBS
- ❏ 2 carrots
- ❏ ½ pointed cabbage (or ½ small green cabbage)
- ❏ 8 small potatoes
- ❏ 2 turnips
- ❏ 1 cos (romaine) lettuce
- ❏ 1 punnet cherry tomatoes

CHILLED PRODUCE
- ❏ ⅓ stewing beef (see week 6)
- ❏ 150 g (5 oz) Comté

GENERAL GROCERIES
- ❏ gherkins (cornichons)

PERSILLADE
- ❏ ½ bunch of flat-leaf parsley
- ❏ ½ bunch of coriander (cilantro) leaves
- ❏ 1 shallot
- ❏ ½ lemon (dash of lemon juice)
- ❏ a little mustard
- ❏ olive oil
- ❏ salt and pepper

Pasta, fennel, orange and cashew salad (week 8)

FRUIT, VEGETABLES AND GENERAL GROCERIES
- ❏ 400 g (14 oz) pasta
- ❏ 100 g (3½ oz/⅔ cup) cashews
- ❏ 4 fennel bulbs
- ❏ 1 tablespoon olive oil
- ❏ 1 orange
- ❏ salt and pepper

YOGHURT DRESSING
- ❏ 300 g (10½ oz/1¼ cups) Greek-style yoghurt
- ❏ 1 garlic clove
- ❏ a little lemon zest
- ❏ ½ lemon (2 teaspoons lemon juice)
- ❏ salt

VINAIGRETTE
- ❏ 1 lemon (2 tablespoons lemon juice)
- ❏ 1 orange (1 tablespoon orange juice)
- ❏ a little lemon zest
- ❏ 1 tablespoon garlic-infused oil (see below)
- ❏ 75 ml (2½ fl oz/5 tablespoons) olive oil
- ❏ salt and pepper

GARLIC OIL
- ❏ 300 ml (10 fl oz/1¼ cups) olive oil
- ❏ 6 garlic cloves
- ❏ 10 basil leaves

Chicken tabbouleh (week 10)

FRUIT, VEGETABLES AND HERBS
- ❏ 1 cucumber
- ❏ 2 bunches of mint
- ❏ 1 bunch of flat-leaf parsley
- ❏ 1 bunch of coriander (cilantro)
- ❏ 2 finely chopped spring onions (scallions)
- ❏ ½ lemon (1 tablespoon lemon juice)

CHILLED PRODUCE
- ❏ 2–3 chicken breasts

GENERAL GROCERIES
- ❏ 150 g (5 oz/scant 1 cup) bulgur
- ❏ ½ tin chickpeas (garbanzos)
- ❏ 1 teaspoon cumin seeds
- ❏ olive oil
- ❏ salt and pepper

DUKKAH
- ❏ 75 g (2½ oz/½ cup) almonds
- ❏ 2 tablespoons coriander seeds
- ❏ 1 tablespoon cumin seeds
- ❏ salt and pepper

Salade Niçoise (week 12)

FRUIT, VEGETABLES AND HERBS
- ❏ 675 g (1 lb 8 oz) fine green beans
- ❏ 2–3 little gem lettuces
- ❏ 500 g (1 lb 2 oz) small potatoes
- ❏ 1 bunch of radishes
- ❏ 500 g (1 lb 2 oz) cherry tomatoes
- ❏ 1 cucumber
- ❏ 3–4 spring onions (scallions)
- ❏ basil

CHILLED PRODUCE
- ❏ 8 eggs

GENERAL GROCERIES
- ❏ 2 x 245 g (5 oz) tins line-caught tuna

VINAIGRETTE
- ❏ 1 garlic clove
- ❏ pinch of lemon zest
- ❏ 1 teaspoon mustard
- ❏ 1½ lemons (3 tablespoons lemon juice)
- ❏ 135 ml (4½ fl oz/9 tablespoons) olive oil

Soups

Squash and sweet potato soup (week 1)

FRUIT, VEGETABLES AND HERBS
- ❏ 2 onions
- ❏ 3 medium sweet potatoes
- ❏ 1 carrot
- ❏ 1 large bunch of flat-leaf parsley

CHILLED PRODUCE
- ❏ 200 ml (7 fl oz/scant 1 cup) full-fat (whole) milk

GENERAL GROCERIES
- ❏ 2 organic vegetable stock cubes
- ❏ olive oil
- ❏ salt and pepper

Lemongrass, coconut, coriander and ginger soup (week 2)

FRUIT, VEGETABLES AND HERBS
- ❏ 1 carrot
- ❏ 2 sticks of lemongrass
- ❏ 1 small chilli
- ❏ 10 cm (4 in) ginger root
- ❏ 2 garlic cloves
- ❏ 2 shallots
- ❏ 2 heads of broccoli (stalks only)
- ❏ 1 bunch of coriander (cilantro) leaves
- ❏ a little mint and coriander (cilantro), to serve

GENERAL GROCERIES
- ❏ 2 organic vegetable stock cubes
- ❏ 200 ml (7 fl oz/scant 1 cup) coconut milk

Cabbage and split pea soup with meatballs (week 3)

4–8 MEATBALLS (SEE WEEK 3)

FRUIT, VEGETABLES AND HERBS
- ❏ ½ heart of pointed cabbage or green cabbage
- ❏ ¼ cauliflower
- ❏ 1 apple
- ❏ 2 sprigs of oregano or thyme
- ❏ 1 bunch of flat-leaf parsley
- ❏ 2 onions
- ❏ 1 garlic clove

GENERAL GROCERIES
- ❏ 120 g (4 oz) split peas
- ❏ 2 organic vegetable or chicken stock cubes

MUSHROOM CONDIMENT
- ❏ 150 g (5 oz) button mushrooms
- ❏ 1 bunch of chives
- ❏ 1 shallot
- ❏ 1 teaspoon grated lemon zest
- ❏ 1 lemon (2 tablespoons lemon juice)
- ❏ 90 ml (3 fl oz/6 tablespoons) olive oil
- ❏ salt and pepper

Cream of vegetable soup (week 4)

FRUIT, VEGETABLES AND HERBS
- ❏ 3 carrots
- ❏ ½ bunch of small turnips (2–3 turnips)
- ❏ 2 small potatoes
- ❏ 2 heads of broccoli (stalks only)
- ❏ 2 leeks
- ❏ ¼ cauliflower
- ❏ 1–2 sprigs of rosemary
- ❏ ½ bunch of chervil, including a few leaves for garnish

CHILLED PRODUCE
- ❏ 750 ml (25 fl oz/3 cups) full-fat (whole) milk
- ❏ 125 ml (4¼ fl oz/½ cup) double (heavy) cream

GENERAL GROCERIES
- ❏ 1 tablespoon olive oil

Watercress soup (week 5)

FRUIT, VEGETABLES AND HERBS
- ❏ 2 red onions
- ❏ 4 potatoes
- ❏ 2 carrots
- ❏ 1 bunch of watercress + the thick stalks of 1 other bunch
- ❏ 1 garlic clove

GENERAL GROCERIES
- ❏ 2 organic chicken stock cubes

POMEGRANATE CONDIMENT
- ❏ 1 pomegranate
- ❏ 1 celery heart
- ❏ 1 small handful of watercress leaves
- ❏ ½–1 small chilli
- ❏ ½ lemon
- ❏ 150 g (5 oz/1 cup) green olives
- ❏ olive oil

Herb and ravioli soup (week 7)

FRUIT, VEGETABLES AND HERBS
- ❏ 2 heads of broccoli (stalks only)
- ❏ 300 g (10½ oz) peas
- ❏ 2 garlic cloves
- ❏ 1 cm (½ in) ginger root
- ❏ ½ bunch of flat-leaf parsley
- ❏ ½ bunch of coriander (cilantro) leaves
- ❏ 150 g (5 oz) rocket (arugula)
- ❏ 1 bunch of dill
- ❏ 5–6 mint leaves

CHILLED PRODUCE
- ❏ 2 packets of ravioli (500 g/1 lb 2 oz)

GENERAL GROCERIES
- ❏ 3 organic vegetable stock cubes
- ❏ 200 ml (7 fl oz/scant 1 cup) double cream or coconut milk

Pea soup (week 8)

FRUIT, VEGETABLES AND HERBS
- ❏ 700 g (1 lb 9 oz) podded peas (can be frozen)
- ❏ ½ bunch of basil

CHILLED PRODUCE
- ❏ 150 g (5 oz/⅔ cup) Greek-style yoghurt

GARLIC OIL
- ❏ 300 ml (10 fl oz/1¼ cups) olive oil
- ❏ 6 garlic cloves
- ❏ 10 basil leaves

Pistou soup (week 9)

FRUIT, VEGETABLES AND HERBS
- ❏ 1–2 onions
- ❏ ½ bunch of small carrots
- ❏ ½ bunch of young turnips
- ❏ ½ bunch of radishes
- ❏ ½ fennel bulb
- ❏ 1 good-sized courgette (zucchini)
- ❏ 250 g (9 oz) Swiss chard

CHILLED PRODUCE
- ❏ 100 g (3½ oz) smoked ham
- ❏ fresh goat's cheese

GENERAL GROCERIES
- ❏ 1–2 tablespoons olive oil
- ❏ 1 organic vegetable or chicken stock cube
- ❏ salt and pepper

PESTO
- ❏ 2–3 bunches of basil
- ❏ 1 bunch of radishes (tops only)
- ❏ 1 tablespoon blanched Swiss chard
- ❏ 2 garlic cloves
- ❏ 100 ml (3½ fl oz/scant ½ cup) olive oil + enough to cover the pesto once stored in the jar
- ❏ 30 g (1 oz) pumpkin seeds
- ❏ salt and pepper

HUMMUS
- ❏ ½ × 400 g (14 oz) tin chickpeas (garbanzos)
- ❏ a little grated lemon zest
- ❏ ½ lemon (2 teaspoons lemon juice)
- ❏ 1 garlic clove
- ❏ a few basil leaves
- ❏ 2 tablespoons olive oil
- ❏ salt and pepper

Gazpacho and hummus (week 10)

FRUIT, VEGETABLES AND HERBS
- ❏ 8 tomatoes
- ❏ 2 cucumbers
- ❏ 2 red (bell) peppers
- ❏ ⅓ bunch of basil
- ❏ 2 tablespoons flat-leaf parsley
- ❏ 2 garlic cloves
- ❏ 3 spring onions

GENERAL GROCERIES
- ❏ olive oil
- ❏ salt and pepper

HUMMUS
- ❏ ½ × 400 g (14 oz) tin chickpeas (garbanzos)
- ❏ ½ lemon (2 teaspoons lemon juice)
- ❏ a little lemon zest
- ❏ 1 tablespoon ground almonds
- ❏ 2 tablespoons olive oil
- ❏ 2 tablespoons coriander (cilantro)
- ❏ 1 garlic clove

DUKKAH
- ❏ 75 g (2½ oz/½ cup) almonds
- ❏ 2 tablespoons coriander seeds
- ❏ 1 tablespoon cumin seeds
- ❏ salt and pepper

Red lentil and coconut milk soup (week 13)

FRUIT, VEGETABLES AND HERBS
- ❏ 4 tomatoes
- ❏ 4 spring onions (scallions)
- ❏ 2 garlic cloves
- ❏ 1 cm (½ in) ginger root
- ❏ ½ lime

GENERAL GROCERIES
- ❏ 300 g (10½ oz/1¼ cups) red lentils
- ❏ 1 cinnamon stick
- ❏ 6 cardamom pods
- ❏ 250 ml (8½ fl oz/1 cup) coconut milk

Pasta & noodles

Tagliatelle with beef sauce, sundried tomatoes and spinach (week 1)
❑ ¼ beef stew (see week 1)

FRUIT, VEGETABLES AND HERBS
❑ handful of flat-leaf parsley

FROZEN PRODUCE
❑ 660 g (2 oz) frozen spinach, defrosted

GENERAL GROCERIES
❑ 400 g (14 oz) tagliatelle
❑ 100 g (3½ oz) sundried tomatoes
❑ 50 g (2 oz/⅓ cup) black olives

Thai noodles (week 2)

FRUIT, VEGETABLES AND HERBS
❑ 2 heads of broccoli (florets only)
❑ 2 carrots
❑ 1 bunch of mint
❑ 1 stick of lemongrass
❑ a little coriander (cilantro)

CHILLED PRODUCE
❑ 3 eggs

GENERAL GROCERIES
❑ 200 g (7 oz) rice noodles, preferably flat
❑ 2 tablespoons oil

PEANUT SAUCE
❑ 1 chilli
❑ 2 shallots
❑ 1 stick of lemongrass
❑ 3 cm (1¼ in) ginger root
❑ 1 garlic clove
❑ 120 ml (4 fl oz/½ cup) cider vinegar
❑ 120 ml (4 fl oz/½ cup) soy sauce
❑ 3 tablespoons caster (superfine) sugar
❑ 2 tablespoons peanut butter

Spaghetti with meatballs (week 3)

FRUIT, VEGETABLES AND HERBS
❑ 3 onions
❑ ½ bunch of flat-leaf parsley
❑ 5 garlic cloves
❑ thyme or oregano
❑ a little flat-leaf parsley
❑ 2 little gem lettuces
❑ a little lemon juice

BAKERY
❑ 120 g (4 oz) stale bread

CHILLED PRODUCE
❑ 500 g (1 lb 2 oz) minced (ground) meat (beef and/or veal and/or pork)
❑ 1 egg
❑ 30 g (1 oz) Parmesan + a little extra to serve

GENERAL GROCERIES
❑ 500 g (1 lb 2 oz) spaghetti or linguine
❑ 2 × 400 g (14 oz) tins chopped tomatoes
❑ 200 ml (7 fl oz/scant 1 cup) passata (sieved tomatoes)
❑ pinch of caster (superfine) sugar
❑ olive oil
❑ salt and pepper

One-pot pasta, cauliflower, lemon, Cheddar and rosemary (week 4)

FRUIT, VEGETABLES AND HERBS
❑ ¾ cauliflower in florets
❑ grated zest of ½ lemon
❑ 2 sprigs of rosemary

CHILLED PRODUCE
❑ 165 g (5½ oz) mild Cheddar

GENERAL GROCERIES
❑ 500 g (1 lb 2 oz) pasta (white or wholemeal)
❑ 2 tablespoons olive oil
❑ salt and pepper

Noodles with vegetables and chicken (week 5)

FRUIT, VEGETABLES AND HERBS
❑ 4 carrots
❑ 300 g (10½ oz) mangetout (snow peas)
❑ ½–1 small chilli
❑ 2 garlic cloves
❑ 1 pomegranate
❑ ½ lemon (1 tablespoon lemon juice)

CHILLED PRODUCE
❑ 1 free-range chicken breast

GENERAL GROCERIES
❑ 300 g (10½ oz) wheat noodles
❑ 2 tablespoons soy sauce
❑ 2 teaspoons caster (superfine) sugar
❑ oil

Noodles in beef stew stock with lemongrass sauce (week 6)

FRUIT, VEGETABLES AND HERBS
❑ a little flat-leaf parsley and coriander (cilantro) for garnish

GENERAL GROCERIES
❑ 300 g (10½ oz) Chinese egg noodles (or soba noodles)
❑ 250–400 ml (8½–13 fl oz) beef stock

LEMONGRASS SAUCE
❑ 1 shallot
❑ ½ bunch of flat-leaf parsley
❑ ½ bunch of coriander (cilantro)
❑ 4 sticks of lemongrass
❑ 2 tablespoons soy sauce
❑ 2 teaspoons caster (superfine) sugar
❑ 2 tablespoons sunflower oil
❑ 2 tablespoons peanut butter

Pasta with garlic-infused oil, cucumber salad and yoghurt dressing (week 8)

FRUIT, VEGETABLES AND HERBS
- ❏ 1 large cucumber (or 2 small ones)
- ❏ basil

GENERAL GROCERIES
- ❏ 600 g (1 lb 5 oz) pasta

YOGHURT DRESSING
- ❏ 300 g (10½ oz/1¼ cups) Greek-style yoghurt
- ❏ 1 garlic clove
- ❏ a little lemon zest
- ❏ ½ lemon (2 teaspoons lemon juice)
- ❏ salt

GARLIC OIL
- ❏ 300 ml (10 fl oz/1¼ cups) olive oil
- ❏ 6 garlic cloves
- ❏ 10 basil leaves

Pasta with pesto (week 9)

CHILLED PRODUCE
- ❏ 100 g (3½ oz) mild Cheddar

GENERAL GROCERIES
- ❏ 500 g (1 lb 2 oz) pasta (spaghetti, for example)
- ❏ pepper

PESTO
- ❏ 2–3 bunches of basil
- ❏ 1 bunch of radishes (tops only)
- ❏ 1 tablespoon blanched Swiss chard
- ❏ 2 garlic cloves
- ❏ 100 ml (3½ fl oz/scant ½ cup) olive oil + enough to cover the pesto once stored in the jar
- ❏ 30 g (1 oz) pumpkin seeds
- ❏ salt and pepper

Summer vegetable pasta (week 10)

FRUIT, VEGETABLES AND HERBS
- ❏ 1 red (bell) pepper
- ❏ 2 courgettes (zucchini)
- ❏ 3 tomatoes

GENERAL GROCERIES
- ❏ 500 g (1 lb 2 oz) pasta
- ❏ 100 g (3½ oz/⅔ cup) pitted olives

CHILLED PRODUCE
- ❏ 40 g (1½ oz) Parmesan

Vegetable lasagne (week 11)

FRUIT, VEGETABLES AND HERBS
- ❏ 10 tomatoes
- ❏ 2 onions
- ❏ 3 garlic cloves
- ❏ 2 aubergines (eggplants)
- ❏ 3 courgettes (zucchini)
- ❏ 1 bunch of basil
- ❏ handful of rocket (arugula)
- ❏ 1 tablespoon flat-leaf parsley
- ❏ 2 teaspoons oregano or thyme
- ❏ 1 lettuce
- ❏ a little lemon juice

CHILLED PRODUCE
- ❏ 250 g (9 oz) mozzarella

GENERAL GROCERIES
- ❏ 500 g (1 lb 2 oz) lasagne sheets
- ❏ 4 tablespoons breadcrumbs
- ❏ olive oil
- ❏ salt and pepper

Olive and goat's cheese pasta (week 12)

FRUIT, VEGETABLES AND HERBS
- ❏ 2–3 spring onions
- ❏ ¼ bunch of flat-leaf parsley

CHILLED PRODUCE
- ❏ 200 g (7 oz) fresh goat's cheese

GENERAL GROCERIES
- ❏ 500 g (1 lb 2 oz) spaghetti
- ❏ 100 g (3½ oz/⅔ cup) black olives
- ❏ 1 tablespoon olive oil
- ❏ salt

Sage ravioli with cucumber (week 12)

FRUIT, VEGETABLES AND HERBS
- ❏ 5–6 sage leaves
- ❏ 1 cucumber
- ❏ flat-leaf parsley

CHILLED PRODUCE
- ❏ 800 g (1 lb 12 oz) fresh ravioli
- ❏ 30 g (1 oz) butter

VINAIGRETTE
- ❏ 1 garlic clove
- ❏ pinch of lemon zest
- ❏ 1 teaspoon mustard
- ❏ 1½ lemons (3 tablespoons lemon juice)
- ❏ 135 ml (4½ fl oz/9 tablespoons) olive oil
- ❏ 1 teaspoon crème fraîche

Carbonara (week 13)

CHILLED PRODUCE
- ❏ 4 egg yolks
- ❏ 40 g (1½ oz) Parmesan + extra to serve
- ❏ 150 g (5 oz) pancetta or lardons

GENERAL GROCERIES
- ❏ 500 g (1 lb 2 oz) pasta

Rice

Risotto (week 6)

FRUIT, VEGETABLES AND HERBS
- ❑ 2 shallots
- ❑ flat-leaf parsley

CHILLED PRODUCE
- ❑ 30 g (1 oz) butter
- ❑ 2 tablespoons crème fraîche
- ❑ 125 g (4 oz) Comté

GENERAL GROCERIES
- ❑ 400 g (14 oz/scant 2 cups) risotto rice
- ❑ 1.2 litres (40 fl oz/4¾ cups) beef stock (or stock cubes + water)
- ❑ 120 ml (4 fl oz/½ cup) white wine
- ❑ 2–3 saffron threads
- ❑ pinch of salt

Rice bowl, roast broccoli and yoghurt dressing (week 7)
- ❑ ½ biryani recipe (see week 7)

FRUIT, VEGETABLES AND HERBS
- ❑ 2 heads of broccoli (florets only)
- ❑ 1 garlic clove
- ❑ a little oregano or thyme

GENERAL GROCERIES
- ❑ 30 g (1 oz/scant ¼ cup) hazelnuts
- ❑ 1 teaspoon garam masala
- ❑ 2 teaspoons olive oil
- ❑ salt

YOGHURT DRESSING
- ❑ 500 g (1 lb 2 oz/2 cups) Greek-style yoghurt
- ❑ zest of 1 lemon
- ❑ 1½ lemons (3 tablespoons lemon juice)
- ❑ 2 garlic cloves
- ❑ a little oregano or thyme
- ❑ salt

Chicken biryani with cranberries (week 7)

FRUIT, VEGETABLES AND HERBS
- ❑ 2 red onions
- ❑ 1 garlic clove
- ❑ 1 cm (½ in) ginger root
- ❑ 200 g (7 oz) podded peas (can be frozen)
- ❑ coriander (cilantro) leaves and flat-leaf parsley

CHILLED PRODUCE
- ❑ 2–3 tikka kebabs
- ❑ 30 g (1 oz) butter
- ❑ 1 tablespoon Greek-style yoghurt

GENERAL GROCERIES
- ❑ 500 g (1 lb 2 oz/2½ cups) basmati rice
- ❑ 70 g (2¼ oz) cranberries
- ❑ 1 tablespoon garam masala
- ❑ 1 organic vegetable stock cube
- ❑ pinch of salt

Rice bowl, courgette fritters and aubergine-yoghurt dressing (week 11)

FRUIT, VEGETABLES AND HERBS
- ❑ 3 courgettes (zucchini)
- ❑ 1 aubergine (eggplant)
- ❑ ½ garlic clove
- ❑ 2½ tablespoons flat-leaf parsley
- ❑ 5–6 basil leaves
- ❑ handful of rocket (arugula)
- ❑ lemon juice and zest

CHILLED PRODUCE
- ❑ 50 g (2 oz) feta
- ❑ 5 eggs
- ❑ 60 g (2 oz) grated Parmesan
- ❑ 150 g (5 oz/⅔ cup) Greek-style yoghurt

GENERAL GROCERIES
- ❑ 300 g (10½ oz/1⅔ cups) long-grain white rice
- ❑ pinch of saffron threads
- ❑ pinch of smoked chilli or paprika
- ❑ olive oil
- ❑ salt and pepper

Fried rice, saffron and apricots with tomato salad (week 11)

FRUIT, VEGETABLES AND HERBS
- ❑ 10 tomatoes
- ❑ 1 aubergine (eggplant)
- ❑ 1–2 onions
- ❑ 1½ garlic cloves
- ❑ 1½ tablespoons chopped flat-leaf parsley
- ❑ 1 lemon (for juice and zest)

CHILLED PRODUCE
- ❑ 150 g (5 oz/⅔ cup) Greek-style yoghurt

GENERAL GROCERIES
- ❑ 300 g (10½ oz/1⅔ cups) long-grain white rice
- ❑ 50 g (2 oz) dried apricots
- ❑ pinch of saffron threads
- ❑ pinch of smoked chilli or paprika
- ❑ 15 g (3 oz) cashews
- ❑ olive oil
- ❑ salt and pepper

Fried rice (week 12)

FRUIT, VEGETABLES AND HERBS
- ❑ 325 g (11 oz) fine green beans
- ❑ 150 g (5 oz) podded peas (can be frozen)
- ❑ 2 cm (¾ in) ginger root
- ❑ 6 garlic cloves
- ❑ basil
- ❑ dash of lemon juice

CHILLED PRODUCE
- ❑ 2 eggs

GENERAL GROCERIES
- ❑ 400 g (14 oz/generous 2 cups) long-grain rice
- ❑ pinch of caster (superfine) sugar
- ❑ 4 tablespoons soy sauce
- ❑ olive oil

Fried rice with chicken (week 13)

FRUIT, VEGETABLES AND HERBS
- ❑ 2 courgettes (zucchini)
- ❑ 2 cm (¾ in) ginger root
- ❑ 4 garlic cloves
- ❑ juice of ½ lime
- ❑ fresh coriander (cilantro) leaves

CHILLED PRODUCE
- ❑ 2 chicken thighs

GENERAL GROCERIES
- ❑ 300 g (10½ oz/1½ cups) rice
- ❑ pinch of sugar
- ❑ 4 tablespoons soy sauce
- ❑ 1 tablespoon olive oil

Meats

Poached chicken breasts, carrots and potatoes with pomegranate condiment (week 5)

FRUIT, VEGETABLES AND HERBS
- ❏ 4 carrots
- ❏ 8 potatoes
- ❏ 3 fennel bulbs

CHILLED PRODUCE
- ❏ 3 chicken breasts

GENERAL GROCERIES
- ❏ 3 organic chicken stock cubes
- ❏ olive oil

POMEGRANATE CONDIMENT
- ❏ 1 pomegranate
- ❏ 1 celery heart
- ❏ 1 small handful of watercress leaves
- ❏ ½–1 small chilli
- ❏ ½ lemon
- ❏ 150 g (5 oz/1 cup) green olives
- ❏ olive oil

Beef stew with persillade (week 6)

FRUIT, VEGETABLES AND HERBS
- ❏ 1 leek
- ❏ 8 carrots
- ❏ 4 turnips
- ❏ 1 celery heart
- ❏ 1 onion
- ❏ 1 bouquet garni (thyme, bay, flat-leaf parsley)
- ❏ 16 small potatoes
- ❏ 1 pointed cabbage (or 1 small green cabbage)

CHILLED PRODUCE
- ❏ 2.5 kg (5 lb 10 oz) stewing beef (ideally a mixture of different cuts: shoulder, shin, best rib, etc. Ask your butcher for advice and include marrowbone if liked.)

GENERAL GROCERIES
- ❏ 10 g (½ oz) peppercorns
- ❏ 2 cloves
- ❏ mustard
- ❏ gherkins (cornichons)

PERSILLADE
- ❏ ½ bunch of flat-leaf parsley
- ❏ ½ bunch of coriander (cilantro)
- ❏ 1 shallot
- ❏ dash of lemon juice
- ❏ a little mustard
- ❏ olive oil
- ❏ salt and pepper

Chicken tikka kebabs with rocket (week 7)

FRUIT, VEGETABLES AND HERBS
- ❏ 2.5 cm (1 in) ginger root
- ❏ 75 g (2½ oz) rocket (arugula)
- ❏ a few mint leaves
- ❏ 1 red onion
- ❏ 1–2 lemons

CHILLED PRODUCE
- ❏ 5 chicken breasts or deboned thighs

GENERAL GROCERIES
- ❏ 1 tablespoon garam masala
- ❏ 1 teaspoon paprika
- ❏ 8–12 pitta breads

YOGHURT DRESSING
- ❏ 500 g (1 lb 2 oz/2 cups) Greek-style yoghurt
- ❏ zest of 1 lemon
- ❏ 1½ lemons (3 tablespoons lemon juice)
- ❏ 2 garlic cloves
- ❏ a little oregano or thyme
- ❏ salt

Stuffed vegetables (week 12)

FRUIT, VEGETABLES AND HERBS
- ❏ 8 tomatoes
- ❏ 8 courgettes (zucchini)
- ❏ 1 red onion
- ❏ ½ bunch of basil
- ❏ ½ bunch of flat-leaf parsley
- ❏ 4 garlic cloves
- ❏ a few sprigs of thyme
- ❏ 2–3 little gem lettuces, to serve

CHILLED PRODUCE
- ❏ 500 g (1 lb 2 oz) sausage meat

GENERAL GROCERIES
- ❏ 2 tablespoons olive oil
- ❏ 50 g (2 oz/¼ cup) long-grain rice
- ❏ salt and pepper

VINAIGRETTE
- ❏ 1 garlic clove
- ❏ pinch of lemon zest
- ❏ 1 teaspoon mustard
- ❏ 1½ lemons (3 tablespoons lemon juice)
- ❏ 135 ml (4½ fl oz/9 tablespoons) olive oil

Roast chicken, vegetables and tortilla wraps (week 13)

FRUIT, VEGETABLES AND HERBS
- ❏ 10 tomatoes
- ❏ 4 courgettes (zucchini)
- ❏ 6 spring onions
- ❏ 6 garlic cloves
- ❏ a few sprigs of thyme

CHILLED PRODUCE
- ❏ 4 chicken drumstick and thighs

GENERAL GROCERIES
- ❏ 12 tortillas (or more, depending on appetite)
- ❏ 300 g (10½ oz/1¾ cups) ready-spiced fine bulgur
- ❏ smoked chilli
- ❏ cumin seeds
- ❏ olive oil
- ❏ salt and pepper

GUACAMOLE
- ❏ 2 avocados
- ❏ juice of ½ lime
- ❏ coriander (cilantro) leaves
- ❏ salt and pepper

TOMATO SALSA
- ❏ 6 tomatoes
- ❏ 2 spring onions (scallions)
- ❏ juice of ½ lime
- ❏ olive oil
- ❏ smoked chilli
- ❏ salt

Fish

Fish gratin with lettuce (week 8)

FRUIT, VEGETABLES AND HERBS
- ❑ 100 g (3½ oz) peas
- ❑ 600 g (1 lb 5 oz) potatoes
- ❑ ½ lettuce of your choice

CHILLED PRODUCE
- ❑ 900 g (2 lb) fish fillets (such as hake)

GENERAL GROCERIES
- ❑ olive oil

VINAIGRETTE
- ❑ 1 lemon (2 tablespoons lemon juice)
- ❑ 1 tablespoon orange juice
- ❑ a little lemon zest
- ❑ 1 tablespoon garlic-infused oil
- ❑ 5 tablespoons olive oil
- ❑ salt and pepper

GARLIC OIL
- ❑ 300 ml (10 fl oz/1¼ cups) olive oil
- ❑ 6 garlic cloves
- ❑ 10 basil leaves

Hake, green beans and radishes with pesto and bulgur (week 9)

FRUIT, VEGETABLES AND HERBS
- ❑ 1 kg (2 lb 4 oz) young green beans
- ❑ ½ bunch of radishes
- ❑ 1 good-sized courgette (zucchini)
- ❑ ½ fennel bulb
- ❑ juice and zest of 1 lemon
- ❑ zest of 1 orange
- ❑ juice of ½ orange
- ❑ basil

CHILLED PRODUCE
- ❑ 600 g (1 lb 5 oz) fresh hake steaks or 1 whole fish (1.2 kg/2lb 10 oz), gutted and scaled

GENERAL GROCERIES
- ❑ 250 g (9 oz/1⅓ cups) coarse bulgur
- ❑ ¼ × 400 g (14 oz) jar passata (sieved tomatoes)
- ❑ 30 g (1 oz) pumpkin seeds
- ❑ a few basil leaves
- ❑ olive oil
- ❑ salt and pepper

PESTO
- ❑ 2–3 bunches of basil
- ❑ 1 bunch of radishes (tops only)
- ❑ 1 tablespoon blanched Swiss chard
- ❑ 2 garlic cloves
- ❑ 100 ml (3½ fl oz/scant ½ cup) olive oil + enough to cover the pesto once stored in the jar
- ❑ 30 g (1 oz) pumpkin seeds
- ❑ salt and pepper

Tuna parcels (week 13)

FRUIT, VEGETABLES AND HERBS
- ❑ ⅓ bunch of coriander (cilantro) leaves
- ❑ 1 cm (½ in) ginger root

CHILLED PRODUCE
- ❑ 200 g (7 oz) fromage frais
- ❑ 1 packet of filo pastry

GENERAL GROCERIES
- ❑ 2 × 145 g (5 oz) tins line-caught tuna in oil
- ❑ olive oil

Stews

Beef stew with potatoes and salad (week 1)

FRUIT, VEGETABLES AND HERBS
- ❏ 2 onions
- ❏ 5 garlic cloves
- ❏ 3 branches of thyme or oregano
- ❏ a few flat-leaf parsley stalks
- ❏ 1 carrot
- ❏ 1 kg (2 lb 4 oz) potatoes
- ❏ ⅓ large lettuce

CHILLED PRODUCE
- ❏ 1.5 kg (3 lb 5 oz) beef: chuck and/or shin (a little more if on the bone), sliced

GENERAL GROCERIES
- ❏ 7 anchovy fillets in oil
- ❏ 2 × 400 g (14 oz) tins peeled or chopped tomatoes
- ❏ 300 ml (10 fl oz/1¼ cups) passata (sieved tomatoes)
- ❏ 100 g (3½ oz/⅔ cup) black olives
- ❏ pinch of caster (superfine) sugar
- ❏ olive oil

Spicy chickpeas, tomatoes and spinach with rice (week 1)

FRUIT, VEGETABLES AND HERBS
- ❏ 2 onions
- ❏ a little flat-leaf parsley

FROZEN
- ❏ 330 g (11 oz) frozen spinach, defrosted

CHILLED PRODUCE
- ❏ 300 g (10½ oz/1¼ cups) Greek-style yoghurt

GENERAL GROCERIES
- ❏ 2 × 400 g (14 oz) tins peeled or chopped tomatoes
- ❏ 2 × 400 g (14 oz) tins chickpeas (garbanzos)
- ❏ 240 g (8½ oz/1¼ cups) basmati rice or long-grain rice
- ❏ 2 teaspoons Indian spice mix (curry, garam masala) + pinch
- ❏ olive oil
- ❏ salt

Vegetable curry with rice (week 4)

FRUIT, VEGETABLES AND HERBS
- ❏ 1 onion
- ❏ 3 cm (1¼ in) ginger root
- ❏ 3 carrots
- ❏ 2 leeks
- ❏ 4 small potatoes
- ❏ ¼ broccoli head
- ❏ 1 pomegranate
- ❏ 1 bunch of coriander (cilantro)

GENERAL GROCERIES
- ❏ 100 g (3½ oz/⅔ cup) almonds
- ❏ 3 tablespoons oil
- ❏ 2 teaspoons Indian spice mix (curry, garam masala)
- ❏ 1 × 250 ml (8½ fl oz/1 cup) tin coconut milk
- ❏ 300 g (10½ oz/1½ cups) long-grain rice
- ❏ 1 teaspoon salt

Vegetable couscous with merguez (week 9)

FRUIT, VEGETABLES AND HERBS
- ❏ 1–2 onions
- ❏ 3–4 cm (1¼–1½ in) ginger root
- ❏ 2 garlic cloves
- ❏ ½ bunch of baby carrots
- ❏ ½ bunch of young turnips
- ❏ ½ bunch of radishes
- ❏ 1 good-sized courgette (zucchini)
- ❏ 2–3 pieces of orange peel

CHILLED PRODUCE
- ❏ 8 merguez sausages

GENERAL GROCERIES
- ❏ 250 g (9 oz/1⅓ cups) coarse bulgur or pre-seasoned couscous
- ❏ 2–3 tablespoons olive oil
- ❏ 2 teaspoons ras el hanout
- ❏ ¾ tin tomato pulp
- ❏ ½ tin chickpeas (garbanzos)
- ❏ 2 organic vegetable or chicken stock cubes
- ❏ a few saffron threads

Tarts & pizzas

Pear and blue cheese mini pizzas with salad (week 2)

FRUIT, VEGETABLES AND HERBS
- ❑ 4 pears
- ❑ 1 lemon
- ❑ 4 tablespoons blanched and chopped Swiss chard
- ❑ 1 large cos (romaine) lettuce

CHILLED PRODUCE
- ❑ 500–600 g (1 lb 2 oz–1 lb 5 oz) pizza dough or 2 ready-made pizza rounds
- ❑ 150 g (5 oz) gorgonzola
- ❑ 1 egg
- ❑ 150 ml (5 fl oz/scant ⅔ cup) crème fraîche

GENERAL GROCERIES
- ❑ 2 tablespoons chopped hazelnuts
- ❑ olive oil
- ❑ nutmeg
- ❑ salt and pepper

Cabbage, fennel and mozzarella pizza (week 3)

FRUIT, VEGETABLES AND HERBS
- ❑ 8 leaves of pointed cabbage or green cabbage
- ❑ 2 little gem lettuces
- ❑ a little lemon juice

CHILLED PRODUCE
- ❑ 500–600 g (1 lb 2 oz–1 lb 5 oz) pizza dough or 2 rounds ready-made pizza dough or 2 packets of puff pastry
- ❑ 300 ml (10 fl oz/1¼ cups) passata (sieved tomatoes)
- ❑ 250 g (9 oz) mozzarella or burrata

GENERAL GROCERIES
- ❑ ½ teaspoon fennel seeds
- ❑ olive oil

MUSHROOM CONDIMENT
- ❑ 150 g (5 oz) button mushrooms
- ❑ 1 bunch of chives
- ❑ 1 shallot
- ❑ 1 teaspoon grated lemon zest
- ❑ 1 lemon (2 tablespoons lemon juice)
- ❑ 90 ml (3 fl oz/6 tablespoons) olive oil
- ❑ salt and pepper

Onion and blue cheese puff pastry tart with watercress salad (week 5)

FRUIT, VEGETABLES AND HERBS
- ❑ 6 red onions
- ❑ 3 sprigs of thyme
- ❑ 1 bunch of watercress leaves
- ❑ a little lemon juice

CHILLED PRODUCE
- ❑ 1 packet of puff pastry
- ❑ 150 g (5 oz) blue cheese

GENERAL GROCERIES
- ❑ olive oil
- ❑ pinch of caster (superfine) sugar
- ❑ salt

POMEGRANATE CONDIMENT
- ❑ 1 pomegranate
- ❑ 1 celery heart
- ❑ 1 small handful of watercress leaves
- ❑ ½–1 small chilli
- ❑ a little lemon juice
- ❑ 150 g (5 oz/1 cup) green olives
- ❑ olive oil

Croque monsieur with salad (week 6)

BAKED GOODS
- ❑ 1 loaf of farmhouse bread, sliced

FRUIT, VEGETABLES AND HERBS
- ❑ 2 onions
- ❑ 1 cos (romaine) lettuce

CHILLED PRODUCE
- ❑ 8 slices of cooked ham
- ❑ 125 g (4 oz) grated Comté
- ❑ 20–30 g (¾–1 oz) butter

GENERAL GROCERIES
- ❑ pinch of salt
- ❑ pinch of caster (superfine) sugar
- ❑ dash of soy sauce

PERSILLADE
- ❑ ½ bunch of flat-leaf parsley
- ❑ ½ bunch of coriander (cilantro) leaves
- ❑ 1 shallot
- ❑ dash of lemon juice
- ❑ a little mustard
- ❑ olive oil
- ❑ salt and pepper

Ham quiche with lettuce (week 8)

FRUIT, VEGETABLES AND HERBS
- ❑ ½ lettuce of your choice

CHILLED PRODUCE
- ❑ 1 packet of shortcrust pastry
- ❑ 3 eggs
- ❑ 200 ml (7 fl oz/scant 1 cup) crème fraîche
- ❑ 300 g (10½ oz/1¼ cups) Greek-style yoghurt
- ❑ 150 g (5 oz) ham (smoked or unsmoked)

GENERAL GROCERIES
- ❑ nutmeg
- ❑ salt and pepper

VINAIGRETTE
- ❑ 1 lemon (2 tablespoons lemon juice)
- ❑ ½ orange (1 tablespoon orange juice)
- ❑ a little lemon zest
- ❑ 75 ml (2½ fl oz/5 tablespoons) olive oil
- ❑ salt and pepper

GARLIC OIL
- ❑ 300 ml (10 fl oz/1¼ cups) olive oil
- ❑ 6 garlic cloves
- ❑ 10 basil leaves

Swiss chard tarts with cherry tomatoes (week 9)

FRUIT, VEGETABLES AND HERBS
- ❑ 750 g (2 oz) Swiss chard
- ❑ 1 garlic clove
- ❑ 2 punnets cherry tomatoes

CHILLED PRODUCE
- ❑ 2 packets of puff pastry
- ❑ 100 g (3½ oz) smoked ham
- ❑ 300 g (10½ oz) Comté or tomme
- ❑ 2 eggs
- ❑ 300 ml (10 fl oz/1¼ cups) crème fraîche

GENERAL GROCERIES
- ❑ olive oil
- ❑ salt and pepper

Gratins

Breads

Autumn-winter gratin with blue cheese (week 2)

FRUIT, VEGETABLES AND HERBS
- ❏ 5 potatoes
- ❏ 1 sweet potato
- ❏ 3 small Swiss chards (or pak choi)
- ❏ 2 shallots
- ❏ 3 garlic cloves
- ❏ a few leaves of cos (romaine) lettuce

CHILLED PRODUCE
- ❏ 100 g (3½ oz) gorgonzola

GENERAL GROCERIES
- ❏ olive oil
- ❏ salt and pepper

Roast autumn vegetables with mozzarella (week 3)

FRUIT, VEGETABLES AND HERBS
- ❏ 1 small butternut squash (about 1 kg/2 lb 4 oz)
- ❏ ¾ cauliflower
- ❏ 4 leaves of pointed cabbage or green cabbage
- ❏ 1 bunch of grapes
- ❏ 4 garlic cloves
- ❏ 4 shallots
- ❏ pinch of oregano

CHILLED PRODUCE
- ❏ 250 g (9 oz) mozzarella or burrata

GENERAL GROCERIES
- ❏ salt and pepper
- ❏ olive oil

MUSHROOM CONDIMENT
- ❏ 150 g (5 oz) button mushrooms
- ❏ 1 bunch of chives
- ❏ 1 shallot
- ❏ 1 teaspoon grated lemon zest
- ❏ 1 lemon (2 tablespoons lemon juice)
- ❏ 6 tablespoons olive oil
- ❏ salt and pepper

Camembert and potatoes with salad (week 4)

FRUIT, VEGETABLES AND HERBS
- ❏ 14 small potatoes
- ❏ 1 cos (romaine) lettuce

CHILLED PRODUCE
- ❏ 1 camembert

GENERAL GROCERIES
- ❏ 1 small glass white wine (optional)
- ❏ salt

VINAIGRETTE
- ❏ zest of ½ lemon
- ❏ 1½ lemons (3 tablespoons lemon juice)
- ❏ 90 ml (3 fl oz/6 tablespoons) olive oil
- ❏ salt and pepper

Broccoli flans with salad (week 4)

FRUIT, VEGETABLES AND HERBS
- ❏ 2 small heads of broccoli (florets only)
- ❏ ½ bunch of chervil
- ❏ 1 cos (romaine) lettuce

CHILLED PRODUCE
- ❏ 4 eggs
- ❏ 250 ml (8½ fl oz/1 cup) cream
- ❏ 250 ml (8½ fl oz/1 cup) full-fat (whole) milk
- ❏ 85 g (3 oz) mild Cheddar or tomme

GENERAL GROCERIES
- ❏ 1 tablespoon olive oil
- ❏ nutmeg
- ❏ salt and pepper

VINAIGRETTE
- ❏ zest of ½ lemon
- ❏ 1½ lemons (3 tablespoons lemon juice)
- ❏ 6 tablespoons olive oil
- ❏ salt and pepper

Gratin with sardines (week 10)

FRUIT, VEGETABLES AND HERBS
- ❏ 10 tomatoes
- ❏ 4 courgettes (zucchini)
- ❏ 2 spring onions (scallions)
- ❏ 1 garlic clove
- ❏ ⅓ bunch of basil

GENERAL GROCERIES
- ❏ tinned sardines
- ❏ olive oil
- ❏ salt and pepper

Garlic bread (week 1)

FRUIT, VEGETABLES AND HERBS
- ❏ ⅓ bunch of flat-leaf parsley
- ❏ 2 garlic cloves

CHILLED PRODUCE
- ❏ 100 g (3½ oz) butter

BAKED GOODS
- ❏ 2 baguettes

Garlic crostini (week 8)

FRUIT, VEGETABLES AND HERBS
- ❏ basil

CHILLED PRODUCE
- ❏ 100 g (3½ oz) cured ham (smoked or unsmoked)
- ❏ 300 g (10½ oz) feta

BAKED GOODS
- ❏ bread

GARLIC OIL
- ❏ 300 ml (10 fl oz/1¼ cups) olive oil
- ❏ 6 garlic cloves
- ❏ 10 basil leaves

Foccacia (week 11)

FRUIT, VEGETABLES AND HERBS
- ❏ 5 slices of roasted aubergine (eggplant)
- ❏ 5 slices of roasted courgette (zucchini)
- ❏ 1 sprig of rosemary

CHILLED PRODUCE
- ❏ 250 g (9 oz) mozzarella
- ❏ 200 g (7 oz/generous ¾ cup) Greek-style yoghurt
- ❏ cold cuts

GENERAL GROCERIES
- ❏ 500 g (1 lb 2 oz/4 cups) plain (all-purpose) flour
- ❏ 15 g (½ oz) fresh baker's yeast or 1 sachet (about 7 g/¼ oz) dried yeast
- ❏ 1 teaspoon salt
- ❏ olive oil
- ❏ sea salt

Eggs

Baked eggs with mushrooms (week 3)

FRUIT, VEGETABLES AND HERBS
- [ ] 350 g (12 oz) button mushrooms
- [ ] 2 shallots
- [ ] 1 tablespoon chopped flat-leaf parsley
- [ ] 1 garlic clove
- [ ] 2 little gem lettuces
- [ ] lemon juice

CHILLED PRODUCE
- [ ] 8 eggs
- [ ] 200 ml (7 fl oz/scant 1 cup) crème fraîche

GENERAL GROCERIES
- [ ] 2 tablespoons olive oil + a little to season the lettuce
- [ ] salt and pepper

Fried eggs, onions and chilli with salad (week 5)

FRUIT, VEGETABLES AND HERBS
- [ ] 4 red onions
- [ ] ½–1 chilli
- [ ] 1 lettuce
- [ ] lemon juice

CHILLED PRODUCE
- [ ] 8 eggs

GENERAL GROCERIES
- [ ] olive oil
- [ ] salt and pepper

Goat's cheese and herb omelette with rocket (week 7)

FRUIT, VEGETABLES AND HERBS
- [ ] 1 bunch of mint
- [ ] 75 g (2½ oz) rocket (arugula)
- [ ] lemon juice

CHILLED PRODUCE
- [ ] 12 eggs
- [ ] 200 g (7 oz) fresh goat's cheese
- [ ] 30 g (1 oz) butter

GENERAL GROCERIES
- [ ] olive oil
- [ ] salt and pepper

Green shakshuka with feta (week 10)

FRUIT, VEGETABLES AND HERBS
- [ ] 3 courgettes (zucchini)
- [ ] 200 g (7 oz) podded peas (can be frozen)
- [ ] ⅓ bunch of basil
- [ ] 2 tablespoons coriander (cilantro) leaves
- [ ] 1 tablespoon flat-leaf parsley

CHILLED PRODUCE
- [ ] 8 eggs
- [ ] 150 g (5 oz) feta

GENERAL GROCERIES
- [ ] 2 tablespoons olive oil

Red shakshuka (week 11)

FRUIT, VEGETABLES AND HERBS
- [ ] 2 red (bell) peppers
- [ ] 10 tomatoes
- [ ] 2 onions
- [ ] 2 garlic cloves
- [ ] 5 basil leaves
- [ ] 150 g (5 oz) rocket (arugula)

CHILLED PRODUCE
- [ ] 8 eggs
- [ ] cold cuts, to serve

GENERAL GROCERIES
- [ ] 1 tablespoon olive oil
- [ ] pinch of smoked chilli or paprika
- [ ] pinch of caster (superfine) sugar

Omelette with buttered radishes (week 13)

FRUIT, VEGETABLES AND HERBS
- [ ] 1 bunch of radishes

CHILLED PRODUCE
- [ ] 12 eggs
- [ ] 100 g (3½ oz) cheese
- [ ] 100 g (3½ oz) butter
- [ ] a little grated Parmesan

GENERAL GROCERIES
- [ ] salt and pepper

Desserts

Crème caramel (week 1)

CHILLED PRODUCE
- [ ] 8 eggs
- [ ] 1 litre (34 fl oz/4 cups) full-fat (whole) milk

GENERAL GROCERIES
- [ ] 350 g (12 oz/1½ cups) caster (superfine) sugar
- [ ] 1 vanilla pod (bean)

Peanut-choc cookies (week 2)

CHILLED PRODUCE
- [ ] 200 g (7 oz) salted butter
- [ ] 2 eggs

GENERAL GROCERIES
- [ ] 200 g (7 oz/scant 1 cup) caster (superfine) sugar
- [ ] 250 g (9 oz/1 cup) peanut butter
- [ ] 340 g (5 oz/2⅔ cups) plain (all-purpose) flour
- [ ] 200 g (7 oz) dark chocolate
- [ ] 120 g (4 oz/1 cup) chopped hazelnuts

Bread pudding (week 3)

CHILLED PRODUCE
- [ ] 100 g (3½ oz) butter
- [ ] 1 litre (34 fl oz/4 cups) full-fat (whole) milk
- [ ] 6 eggs

BAKED GOODS
- [ ] 1 stale baguette

GENERAL GROCERIES
- [ ] 50 g (2 oz/¼ cup) caster (superfine) sugar
- [ ] marmalade

Baked apples (week 4)

FRUIT, VEGETABLES AND HERBS
- [ ] 12 apples
- [ ] juice of ½ lemon

CHILLED PRODUCE
- [ ] butter
- [ ] 125 ml (4¼ fl oz/½ cup) cream

GENERAL GROCERIES
- [ ] 50 g (2 oz/⅓ cup) almonds
- [ ] 4 tablespoons honey
- [ ] nutmeg

Pancakes (week 5)

CHILLED PRODUCE
- ❏ 4 eggs
- ❏ 500 ml (17 fl oz/2 cups) full-fat (whole) milk
- ❏ butter

GENERAL GROCERIES
- ❏ 400 g (14 oz/3¼ cups) plain (all-purpose) flour
- ❏ 21 g (¾ oz) baking powder
- ❏ 2 tablespoons caster (superfine) sugar
- ❏ maple syrup, to serve
- ❏ salt

Shortbread biscuits (week 6)

FRUIT, VEGETABLES AND HERBS
- ❏ zest of 1 lemon

CHILLED PRODUCE
- ❏ 200 g (7 oz) butter

GENERAL GROCERIES
- ❏ 300 g (10½ oz/2½ cups) plain (all-purpose) flour
- ❏ 90 g (3¼ oz/⅓ cup) caster (superfine) sugar
- ❏ pinch of salt

Granola (week 7)

FRUIT, VEGETABLES AND HERBS
- ❏ a little lemon and orange zest
- ❏ fresh fruit

CHILLED PRODUCE
- ❏ yoghurt

GENERAL GROCERIES
- ❏ 300 g (10½ oz/2 cups) oat flakes
- ❏ 2 tablespoons olive oil
- ❏ 2 tablespoons honey
- ❏ 90 g (3¼ oz/⅔ cup) hazelnuts
- ❏ 2 tablespoons selected seeds
- ❏ 2 tablespoons grated coconut (optional)
- ❏ 125 g (4 oz) cranberries
- ❏ pinch of salt

Scones (week 8)

FRUIT, VEGETABLES AND HERBS
- ❏ 1 teaspoon lemon and orange zest

CHILLED PRODUCE
- ❏ 100 g (3½ oz) butter
- ❏ 200 ml (7 fl oz/scant 1 cup) full-fat (whole) milk
- ❏ butter

GENERAL GROCERIES
- ❏ 400 g (14 oz/3¼ cups) plain (all-purpose) flour
- ❏ 60 g (2 oz/¼ cup) caster (superfine) sugar
- ❏ 7 g (¼ oz) baking powder
- ❏ pinch of salt
- ❏ jam (jelly)

Baked rhubarb (week 9)

FRUIT, VEGETABLES AND HERBS
- ❏ 1 kg (2 lb 4 oz) rhubarb
- ❏ zest of ½ orange
- ❏ 2 tablespoons orange juice

CHILLED PRODUCE
- ❏ crème fraîche, soft white cheese or yoghurt

GENERAL GROCERIES
- ❏ 150 g (5 oz/⅔ cup) caster (superfine) sugar

Raspberry clafoutis (week 10)

FRUIT, VEGETABLES AND HERBS
- ❏ 300 g (10½ oz) raspberries (may be frozen)

CHILLED PRODUCE
- ❏ 400 ml (13 fl oz/generous 1½ cups) crème fraîche
- ❏ 400 ml (13 fl oz/generous 1½ cups) full-fat (whole) milk
- ❏ 8 eggs
- ❏ 10 g (½ oz) butter for the dish

GENERAL GROCERIES
- ❏ 75 g (2½ oz/scant ⅔ cup) plain (all-purpose) flour
- ❏ 75 g (2½ oz/⅓ cup) caster (superfine) sugar + a little to sprinkle over the raspberries
- ❏ 2 tablespoons Grand Marnier
- ❏ 2 tablespoons ground almonds

Milkshake (week 11)

FRUIT, VEGETABLES AND HERBS
- ❏ 500 g (1 lb 2 oz) strawberries
- ❏ a few basil leaves (optional)

CHILLED PRODUCE
- ❏ 300 g (10½ oz/1¼ cups) Greek-style yoghurt
- ❏ 250 ml (8½ fl oz/1 cup) vanilla ice cream

Roast fruit (week 12)

FRUIT, VEGETABLES AND HERBS
- ❏ 2 kg (4 lb 8 oz) mixture of peaches, plums and apricots
- ❏ some lemon peel and zest

CHILLED PRODUCE
- ❏ crème fraîche

GENERAL GROCERIES
- ❏ 1–2 tablespoons caster (superfine) sugar

Pear brownies (week 13)

CHILLED PRODUCE
- ❏ 200 g (7 oz) butter
- ❏ 4 eggs

GENERAL GROCERIES
- ❏ 250 g (9 oz) chocolate
- ❏ 225 g (8 oz/1 cup) caster (superfine) sugar
- ❏ 130 g (4½ oz/1 cup) plain (all-purpose) flour
- ❏ 400 g (14 oz) pears in syrup

INDEX

A
anchovies
Caesar salad with garlic bread 12

apple
Baked apples 48

aubergines
Focaccia with lettuce 132
Rice bowl, courgette fritters and
    aubergine-yoghurt dressing 132

B
beef
Beef stew with persillade 72
Beef stew with potatoes and salad 12
Next-day beef stew salad 72
Noodles in beef stew stock with
    lemongrass sauce 72
Spaghetti with meatballs 36
Tagliatelle with beef sauce, sundried
    tomatoes and spinach 12

broccoli
Big broccoli and lentil salad with peanut
    dressing 24
Broccoli flans with salad 48
Rice bowl, roast broccoli and yoghurt
    dressing 84
Thai noodles 24

bulgur
Chicken tabbouleh 120
Hake, green beans and radishes with
    pesto and bulgur 108
Vegetable couscous and merguez 108

butternut
Poached chicken breasts, carrot and potatoes
    with pomegranate condiment 60

C
cabbage
Beef stew with persillade 72
Cabbage and split pea soup with meatballs 36
Cabbage, fennel and mozzarella pizza 36
Next-day beef stew salad 72
Roast autumn vegetables with mozzarella 36

carrot
Cream of vegetable soup 48
Noodles with vegetables and chicken 60
Roast autumn vegetables with mozzarella 36
Vegetable couscous and merguez 108
Vegetable curry with rice 48

cashews
Fried rice, saffron and apricots with
    tomato salad 132
Pasta, fennel, orange and cashew salad 96

cauliflower
Cabbage and split pea soup with
    meatballs 36
One-pot pasta, cauliflower, lemon,
    Cheddar and rosemary 48
Roast autumn vegetables with mozzarella 36

cheese
Croque monsieur with salad 72
Camembert and potatoes with salad 48
Omelette with buttered radishes 156
One-pot pasta, cauliflower, lemon,
    Cheddar and rosemary 48
Pear and blue cheese mini pizzas with
    salad 24
Risotto 72

cherry tomatoes
Salade Niçoise 144
Swiss chard tarts with cherry tomatoes 108

chicken
Chicken biryani with cranberries 84
Chicken tabbouleh 120
Chicken tikka kebabs with rocket 84
Fried rice with chicken 156
Noodles with vegetables and chicken 60
Poached chicken breasts, carrots and
    potatoes with pomegranate
    condiment 60
Roast chicken, vegetables and tortilla
    wraps 156

chickpeas
Chicken tabbouleh 120
Hummus 108
Spicy chickpeas, tomatoes and spinach
    with rice 12
Vegetable couscous with merguez 108

chocolate
Peanut-choc cookies 24
Pear brownies 156

coconut milk
Lemongrass, coconut, coriander and
    ginger soup 24
Red lentil and coconut milk soup with
    tuna parcels 156

cold cuts
Carbonara 156
Croque monsieur with salad 72
Ham quiche with lettuce 96
Swiss chard tarts with cherry tomatoes 108

coriander
Lemongrass, coconut, coriander and
    ginger soup 24

courgette
Gratin with sardines 120
Green shakshuka with feta 120
Rice bowl, courgette fritters and
    aubergine-yoghurt dressing 132
Stuffed vegetables 144
Summer vegetable pasta 120

cucumber
Chicken tabbouleh 120
Gazpacho and hummus 120
Salade Niçoise 144

F
fennel
Cabbage, fennel and mozzarella pizza 36
Pasta, fennel, orange and cashew salad 96

fish
Fish gratin with lettuce 96
Hake, green beans and radishes with
    pesto and bulgur 108

fruit
Milkshake 132
Raspberry clafoutis 120
Roast autumn vegetables with mozzarella 36
Roast fruit 144

G
garlic
Garlic bread 12
Pasta with garlic-infused oil, cucumber
    salad and yoghurt dressing 96
Pea soup with garlic crostini 96

ginger
Lemongrass, coconut, coriander and
    ginger soup 24

goat's cheese
Goat's cheese and herb omelette with
    rocket 84
Olive and goat's cheese pasta with
    buttered radishes 144

green beans
Avocado and fried rice 144
Hake, green beans and radishes with
  pesto and bulgur 108
Salade Niçoise 144

L
leek
Beef stew with persillade 72
Cream of vegetable soup 48
Vegetable curry with rice 48

lemongrass
Lemongrass, coconut, coriander and
  ginger soup 24
Noodles in beef stew stock with
  lemongrass sauce 72

lentils
Big broccoli and lentil salad with peanut
  dressing 24
Red lentil and coconut milk soup with
  tuna parcels 156

M
mozzarella
Cabbage, fennel and mozzarella pizza 36
Roast autumn vegetables with mozzarella 36

mushrooms
Baked eggs with mushrooms 36
Mushroom condiment 36

O
orange
Pasta, fennel, orange and cashew salad 96

P
peanut butter
Peanut-choc cookies 24
Peanut dressing 24

peas
Fish gratin with lettuce 96
Green shakshuka with feta 120
Herb and ravioli soup 84
Pea soup with garlic crostini 96

peppers
Gazpacho and hummus 120
Red shakshuka 132
Summer vegetable pasta 120

pomegranate
Pomegranate condiment 60

potatoes
Beef stew with persillade 72
Beef stew with potatoes and salad 12
Fish gratin with lettuce 96
Camembert and potatoes with salad 48
Next-day beef stew salad 72
Poached chicken breasts, carrots and
  potatoes with pomegranate
  condiment 60
Salade Niçoise 144

R
rhubarb
Baked rhubarb 108

S
sage
Sage ravioli with cucumber 144

sausage meat
Stuffed vegetables 144
Vegetable couscous with merguez 108

spinach
Spicy chickpeas, tomatoes and spinach
  with rice 12
Tagliatelle with beef sauce, sundried
  tomatoes and spinach 12

split peas
Cabbage and split pea soup with
  meatballs 36

squash
Potimarron squash and sweet potato
  soup with garlic bread 12

sweet potato
Autumn-winter gratin with blue cheese 24
Squash and sweet potato
  soup with garlic bread 12

Swiss chard
Autumn-winter gratin with blue cheese 24
Pasta with pesto 108
Pear and blue cheese mini pizzas
  with salad 24
Pistou soup 108
Swiss chard tarts with cherry tomatoes 108

T
tomato
Fried rice, saffron and apricots with
  tomato salad 132
Gazpacho and hummus 120
Gratin with sardines 120

Stuffed vegetables 144
Summer vegetable pasta 120
Tomato salsa 156
Vegetable lasagne 132

tuna
Red lentil and coconut milk soup with
  tuna parcels 156
Salade Niçoise 144

turnip
Beef stew with persillade 72
Cream of vegetable soup 48
Next-day beef stew salad 72
Pistou soup 108
Vegetable couscous with merguez 108

W
watercress
Onion and blue cheese puffed pastry tart
  with watercress salad 60
Watercress soup 60

Y
yoghurt
Fried rice, saffron and apricots with
  tomato salad 132
Milkshake 132
Pea soup with garlic crostini 96
Spicy chickpeas, tomatoes and spinach
  with rice 12
Yoghurt dressing 84, 96

Thank you!

To Christine, Élise, Pierre, Orathay and Rosemarie.

First published by Marabout in 2018
Published in 2019 by Hardie Grant Books,
an imprint of Hardie Grant Publishing

Hardie Grant Books (London)
5th & 6th Floors
52–54 Southwark Street
London SE1 1UN

Hardie Grant Books (Melbourne)
Building 1, 658 Church Street
Richmond, Victoria 3121

hardiegrantbooks.com

British Library Cataloguing-in-Publication Data. A catalogue record for
this book is available from the British Library.

Batch Cooking by Keda Black
ISBN: 978-1-78488-275-4

Design: Christine Legeret and Orathay Souksisavanh
Photography: Pierre Javelle
Graphic design and layout: Sophie Villette
Pictograms: © Shutterstock

For the English edition:
Publishing Director: Kate Pollard
Junior Editor: Eila Purvis
Translator: Gilla Evans
Typesetter: David Meikle
Editor: Sarah Herman
Proofreader: Kay Delves

Colour reproduction by p2d
Printed and bound in China by Leo Paper Products Ltd.

Date:

Contents:

Eating day:

Date:

Contents:

Eating day:

Date:

Contents:

Eating day:

Date:

Contents:

Eating day:

Date:

Contents:

Eating day:

Date:

Contents:

Eating day:

Date:

Contents:

Eating day:

Date:

Contents:

Eating day:

Date:

Contents:

Eating day:

Date:

Contents:

Eating day:

Date:

Contents:

Eating day:

Date:

Contents:

Eating day: